Endorsements

"As leaders, we all are seeking that special secret that will allow us to achieve balance in our lives. In *Awaken the Leader in You*, Linda Clark gives a refreshing look at ten life essentials affecting leadership and offers biblical foundations and practical, easy-to-understand suggestions of ways for the leader to adjust her thinking in order to find balance. *Awaken the Leader in You* is also filled with stories a leader can relate to and in which she can see herself involved. This book is a must-read for anyone who wears more than one hat!"

—**Kimberly K. Runner**, missions education and women's ministry strategist, Northwest Baptist Convention

"*Awaken the Leader in You* is a timely addition to resources available for women in leadership and for those who desire to engage women in discovering their leadership potential. Dr. Linda Clark presents a thought-provoking, user-friendly approach in her presentation of the essential areas of a woman's life, all the while balancing biblical foundations with the humor of daily life experiences. Well-written, real, and applicable for all women desiring to develop a spiritually balanced life and bring others along on the journey. The study guide option for women's small groups at the conclusion of the work adds to the value."

—**Eva De La Rosa**, adjunct professor, Golden Gate Baptist Theological Seminary

Awaken the LEADER *in* YOU

10 Life Essentials *for* Women *in* Leadership

by

DR. LINDA M. CLARK

NEW HOPE
PUBLISHERS

Birmingham, Alabama

New Hope® Publishers
P. O. Box 12065
Birmingham, AL 35202-2065
www.newhopepublishers.com

New Hope Publishers is a division of WMU®.

Library of Congress Cataloging-in-Publication Data

Clark, Linda M.
  Awaken the leader in you : 10 life essentials for women in leadership
/ by Linda Clark.
     p. cm.
  ISBN 978-1-59669-221-3 (sc)
  1. Leadership--Religious aspects--Christianity. 2. Christian women.
I. Title.
  BV4597.53.L43C53 2009
  248.8'43--dc22

                              2008041408

ISBN-10: 1-59669-221-9
ISBN-13: 978-1-59669-221-3
N084144 • 0309 • 3M1

Dedicated to Donna whose too-short life
demonstrated that Christian women
can be influential leaders
when they live and lead in balance.

Table of Contents

Acknowledgments

No book is printed all on its own! Nor is it written in isolation. Such certainly is the case with *Awaken the Leader in You*. While the idea surfaced in my mind, the end result is the joint effort of many.

Special thanks go to my husband, Jan, as his support is constant and encouraging. His willingness to read rough drafts, more drafts, and final drafts is evidence of his commitment to me, my ministry, and this project.

My strongest source of encouragement has been my parents, William and Wilma Bell, as they first instilled the love of reading in me at an early age. They have always received my writing efforts with enthusiasm and have never failed to cheer me on. My mother has read this entire manuscript, magnifying glass in hand, and deemed it "good advice for today's women."

The women with whom I have worked in my current ministry position for the past 13 years have directed what I have written. Their lives, ministries, and commitment to leadership have motivated me to tell their stories and demonstrate the need for Christian women to develop their leadership skills for God's kingdom service.

Leaders who have moved in and out of my life certainly influenced my thoughts as I penned this book. Their dedication to continued learning and to developing their God-given potential spurred me on to produce a book that will guide women in their leadership journeys. Among others stand Ethel McIndoo, who always has a word of encouragement; Debra Bell, now with the Lord still saying, "You go, girl"; Mike McCullough, my insightful supervisor; Paula Case, my former business partner; and Diane Varady, who has listened to all my writer's woes.

An idea is born not in a vacuum but within our heart's desire. The desire to equip women with the tools they need for successful leadership remains a motivating force behind much of what I do in ministry. God has placed that desire in my heart and until He moves me to another area, I will continue to write and speak about leadership at every opportunity, because I truly believe He wants you to *"do what you can, not what you can't. The heart regulates the hands"* (2 Corinthians 8:10–11 *The Message*).

Introduction
Achieving Balance in Your Life as a Leader

I tried doing at home what she does in her TV kitchen. Now, I'm not terribly interested in cooking (I officially closed my kitchen several years ago), but I thought I might be able to carry as many things from the refrigerator and pantry as she does. After all it was just juggling a lot of things at one time—the ability to achieve a balance between the potatoes, the fresh parsley, the seasonings, butter, a large onion, oh, and yes, the two bowls, a package of meat, and mushrooms on top of a serving platter. No problem, right? Well, I soon discovered my sense of balance is obviously not as well developed as Rachael Ray's!

Balance isn't just a matter of juggling culinary items nor is it learning to walk across a tightrope. It is now a topic bandied about in women's magazines, on television documentaries, and even in newspapers. Countless books give women suggestions and encouragement to develop somehow from within themselves a sense of balance. Could it be that the reason we read and hear so much about balance is that so few have achieved it?

Women often find themselves wedged between obligations, needs, and dreams. The obligations race to the forefront of a woman's life and can consume all of her waking hours. Her needs may very well get lost in the shuffle of day-to-day activities such as childcare, career, home maintenance, dentist and doctor appointments, community events, and church responsibilities. Does any of that sound familiar? Then, there are the dreams. Many youthful dreams have become distant memories. Dreams of higher education; dreams of world travel; dreams of position and influence; or dreams of self-employment are tucked away and rarely looked at. When a woman's obligations, needs, and dreams collide, the result is all too often a life that is neither balanced nor fulfilling.

In my ministry I've found that women identify four issues as major concerns. Stop a minute and think about the areas of your life that seem to be spiraling out of control. Are any of these issues concerns for you?

- *There is no time to do it all.* This is a common problem, and one that creates a great deal of stress.
- *I feel so guilty.* Whatever their responsibilities, women often feel they what they are doing is inadequate and incomplete. Whether it is working at home, at church, in the neighborhood or community, or in the office, women feel they are short-changing everyone.
- *Take care of myself? Sure! Where does that fit into an already too-tight schedule?* Some women consider this as an impossibility.
- *I'm a basket case and see no way out.* When women feel dry emotionally and spiritually, real trouble is waiting in the wings.

These concerns are very revealing as they are an indication that women are aware of the magnitude of their dilemma but at the same time realize they do not have the solutions to better their situation.

If achieving balance in life is so difficult for everyone, how can a woman in leadership find it? And that brings us to this question: is there a connection between balance and effective leadership?

There are all kinds of (false) formulas for creating balance in one's life. New Age proponents tell readers to get in touch with their inner self. Feminists assure women all their problems can be laid at men's feet. Some authors assert that if a woman really wants to do something, nothing can stop her.

Women who desire to become better leaders by fine-tuning their leadership skills may have difficulty in finding reliable sources to help. The purpose of this book is to provide just such a resource from a Christian perspective. If you are interested in expanding your understanding of leadership principles, this book is for you! Having balance in your life is key to being an effective leader whether it is in the context of your family, in your neighborhood, in the workplace, or in your church.

Awaken the Leader in You examines ten life essentials that will give you a better grasp on issues affecting your leadership roles. Every woman needs to achieve balance in these areas and understand their influences on her leadership capabilities. Each chapter examines how one of these life essentials relates to leadership and includes a biblical foundation and practical suggestions for reaching balance.

In each chapter you will also find:

- Equipoise (balance)—applications to leadership.
- God's Symmetry—a taste of what God's Word says about the topic.
- Tipping the Scales—ideas, tips, suggestions specifically related to the chapter subject.
- Notes—A space to reflect on the chapter's meaning for you.

Finally, the book concludes with a group study guide. For use by small group leaders, the guide includes enhancer ideas, which provide creative ideas for studying and discussing the material found in the different chapters. Each chapter references an "object" that can be used to create interest in the chapter subject.

Equilibrium, steadiness, harmony, proportion, compatibility, amity, refinement, erudition, knowledge. Until we as women learn to achieve balance in our lives and develop as leaders in the way God intends, these are just words. We'll try to juggle our various activities, our very lives—like Rachael Ray juggles her kitchen supplies—but we'll never achieve balance. However, when we evaluate where we need to change and gain an understanding of how God will transform our lives, we can put our lives and hearts in order as women and as leaders.

1

What Do Spuds Have to Do with My Life?

◇◇◇◇◇◇◇◇

A leader of good judgment gives stability.
—Proverbs 29:4

◇◇◇◇◇◇◇◇

Awaken the Leader in You

Other than peeling them for dinner, what could potatoes have to do with the life of a woman seeking balance?

Potatoes have long been regarded as one of life's staples, a foundation if you will. They can be scalloped, smashed, baked, or fried, among other things. They are basic, simple fare, but oh, so welcome! Regardless of their starch and calories, they have carved out for themselves a permanent place in the American diet.

I grew up in a pastor's home, and while we always had enough food, it was simple fare. My father was a meat-and-potatoes man who never ate fish or fowl. Before I left home for college, we did have an occasional taco, but Chinese food, tuna salads, or more exotic culinary dishes were never seen on our table.

My brother is a vegetarian, so my mother used potatoes in a variety of ways. When it became fashionable to eat rice, we occasionally had Rice-A-Roni. Today, while we know all about starch and its effect on our bodies, my family members are still very big fans of potatoes. We like them diced, chopped, sliced, mashed, and fried. You mention potato, and we order it in some form with our meals!

A parallel can be drawn from the ever-popular potato to our spiritual lives. Just as the potato may be a dietary staple, one's spiritual foundation (staple) determines the direction that a person's life will take. If a woman desires to find balance in her life, she must come to realize that true life, lived to its fullest, comes through a relationship with Jesus Christ.

That relationship begins when a person trusts Jesus and accepts what He did for us when He died on the Cross for our sins. The psalmist says, *"Soak me in your laundry and I'll come out clean; scrub me and I'll have a snow-white life"* (Psalm 51:7). A woman seeking balance in her life must stop here first. Life itself will have little meaning apart from a relationship with God. Romans 5:18 states, *"More than just getting us out of trouble, he got us into life!"*

Of course, having a personal relationship with Christ is not a blank check that guarantees we will no longer struggle with balance issues! It does not guarantee that we will be better managers of our time. It does not mean we will be able to say no to lesser things, or be more successful in achieving our goals. It does, however, give us that basic foundation for living our lives without fear of the future. The writer of Proverbs tells us, *"You can't find firm footing in a swamp; but life rooted in God stands firm"* (Proverbs 12:3). If we are to live balanced lives, we'll need that firm footing.

During the Great Depression, the potato was an available and affordable commodity. It stretched many meals and filled many hungry stomachs during those lean years. In the back of every cook's mind was the thought, *I can always rely on potatoes.* A relationship with Jesus that acknowledges Him as Savior and Lord provides a firm footing that we can always rely on. Our ineptitude in scheduling our time, fulfilling our responsibilities, and reaching our goals does not change what Jesus did for us on the Cross. Nor does it have anything to do with *what* we do. Better written would be what *we* do. *"We are saved through the grace (the undeserved favor and mercy) of the Lord Jesus"* (Acts 15:11 AMP). There is nothing we can do to earn or deserve what Jesus did for us through His perfect life on earth and His death on the Cross.

Let's look at a snapshot of a woman changed by Jesus.

━ Biblical Snapshot ━

Acts 16:8–14 gives the account of Paul and his companions trying to travel to Asia (a part of Turkey today) to proclaim the good news there. Redirected by the Holy Spirit, they went down to the city of Troas, which was on the coast of the Adriatic Sea. Troas today is called Eski-Stambul. While there, Paul had a vision of a man calling him to come to Macedonia (now Eastern Europe). Not a person to let the grass grow under his feet, Paul decided this vision was from God and sailed across to Samothrace. After landing, he and his companions went to Neapolis (now a holiday resort city).

Paul and his friends eventually arrived in Philippi, a good destination because it was an influential city in that day. Macedonia was a Roman colony and was a strategic place for them to begin to proclaim the gospel. The people were already having prayer meetings at the river's edge. Luke, the author of Acts, does not say how Paul knew the people were having prayer meetings. Perhaps he found out that there were no synagogues in Philippi and asked where they were meeting. Or, perhaps he heard about the meetings from a merchant in the marketplace.

When the men reached the spot they had been told about, they found a group of women gathered to pray. Lydia, a seller of purple cloth, was among the women. She may have been their leader. Evidently, Lydia had converted to Judaism and worshipped God. As Paul told her and the others about the Messiah, *"the Lord opened her heart"* (Acts 16:14 AMP). Lydia moved from being a worshipper to having a personal relationship with Christ. She, in fact, was the first convert in Europe.

She also must have been an astute businesswoman, since the production and sale of purple cloth was a lucrative trade. Many Bible scholars believe she was a widow who used her skills to provide for her family. The dyeing process for purple cloth was a carefully guarded secret, so it could be that Lydia's husband (assuming she was married) first knew the secret, and upon his death, she took over the business.

In this snapshot, we find a woman who was accomplished in many ways. She was financially secure, evidently confident of her abilities, and sought to please God through her worship. She was lacking something, however. She did not have the basic staple in her life that would assure her of her eternal future. Her recognition that Jesus was indeed the long-awaited Messiah became the turning point in her successful life. Her reason for living became a desire to learn more about Him and find His direction for her life.

Lydia's relationship with Jesus also motivated her to step forward and to become a member of Paul's evangelism team in Europe. We'll see later how her salvation experience led her into new areas of ministry, helping her to achieve greater balance in her life as a Christian woman.

A Firm Foundation

It could be that as you are reading you wonder whether you have Christ as the foundation of your life. The Bible clearly reveals to us how to take that first step. If this discussion has brought doubts about a personal relationship with Christ to your mind, please read the following passages, and then, trust Him for the peace, forgiveness, and life only He can give. Without Him, your life will never be in balance. If you already live with the assurance of Christ in your heart, reread these familiar verses and make the commitment to share them with someone at work, in your neighborhood, or family who needs to hear about the joy that comes by answering God's call to come to Him.

> *Since all have sinned and are falling short of the honor and glory which God bestows and receives. [All] are justified and made upright and in right standing with God . . . through the redemption which is [provided] in Christ Jesus.*
> —Romans 3:23-24 (AMP)

> *For the wages which sin pays is death; but the [bountiful] free gift of God is eternal life through (in union with) Jesus Christ our Lord."*
> —Romans 6:23 (AMP)

> *Because if you acknowledge and confess with your lips that Jesus is Lord and in your heart believe (adhere to, trust in, and rely on the truth) that God raised Him from the dead, you will be saved.*
> —Romans 10:9 (AMP)

You might pray this prayer right now: *God, I admit that the sin in my life has separated me from You. I know that Jesus died for my sins and that He is able to intervene for me with You. I accept the sacrifice He made for me and want Him to bring freedom and peace into my life. I ask that you accept me because of what Jesus did for me.*

Leadership Basics

Because a salvation experience (establishing a personal relationship with Jesus) is foundational to one's life, it also affects a person's ability to lead. The Book of Proverbs is a virtual gold mine of statements about leadership and descriptions of the Christian leader. It outlines the characteristics of a good leader and shows how the world views leaders. The following are a few examples of how a Christian leader needs to behave and relate to her followers:

The mark of a good leader is loyal followers; leadership is nothing without a following.
—Proverbs 14:28

A good leader motivates, doesn't mislead, doesn't exploit.
—Proverbs 16:10

Good leaders cultivate honest speech; they love advisors who tell them the truth.
—Proverbs 16:13

We don't expect eloquence from fools, nor do we expect lies from our leaders.
—Proverbs 17:7

Love and truth form a good leader; sound leadership is founded on loving integrity.
—Proverbs 20:28

Good leadership is a channel of water controlled by God; he directs it to whatever ends he chooses.
—Proverbs 21:1

Back to the potato…even with its starch content, the potato is regarded as a staple of life (more for some people than others). Leadership also has "staples." A Christian leader must possess certain elements in order to be an effective leader. While not all of the elements will be discussed in detail in this chapter, let's take a brief look at them, as they are the foundation for balanced leadership.

A balanced leader with a personal relationship with Jesus should have **integrity**. This means being honest, upright, truthful, and reliable. When a woman seeks to lead with integrity, the decisions she makes and the way she relates to others will be filtered through her relationship with Christ. For *Women, Faith, and Work*, Lois Flowers interviewed women who have integrated their faith in Jesus into every aspect of their lives. God's call on their lives influences the decisions they make. For instance, Jeannette Towne, owner of her own communications company, believes the way she relates to others must be an indication of her trust in God. She values her integrity because she wants it to be a reflection of her relationship with Jesus. William Woodfin, former pastor of Edgewater Presbyterian Church in Chicago, said, "The proof of Christianity is not a book but a life."

Service is another element a balanced leader should seek. A lot has been written about servant leadership. The issue is not what we know, but what we do about it. A **servant outlook** should be noticeable in a leader's life and approach to her role as a leader. For *Women, Faith, and Work*, Lois Flowers interviewed Allyson Hodgins, a woman whose career, a very lucrative one, was in management consultation. She was a member of a mission team who went to Romania. While there, her heart was touched by the thousands of orphans. She believed there was something she could do. Gathering supporters with the same commitment, she formed a nonprofit organization to establish orphanages. She worked out a plan with her company to allow her to cut her work year from 12 months to 8, enabling her to travel and work to create safe havens for orphans. Her business acumen has allowed her not only to use her skills but to help others to develop sound business procedures. She saw tremendous need, was convicted that she could do something about that need, and made decisions that allowed her to have an ongoing part in providing shelter and care for orphan children. She practices servant leadership.

Accountability is a word that most of us don't like. It smacks of doing something we aren't really sure we want to do, for longer than we want to, with uncertain results! This word carries with it the concept of being responsible and reliable. And, if a woman wants balance in her leadership role, whatever that is, she must be accountable.

You may say, "Well, I don't have any real leadership position so I can skip this part." Every woman is a leader in some capacity. The issue becomes not whether we are or are not leaders, but the degree to which we regard accountability as something important in our lives. If you are a leader in your family, as a volunteer at the county library, if you work part time as a retail salesperson, or if you hold a supervisory position with a corporation, accountability is required of you. As Christian leaders we are held accountable for the way we lead and how we treat others in the process. *"All the ways of a man are pure in his own eyes, but the Lord weighs the spirits (the thoughts and intents of the heart)"* (Proverbs 16:2 AMP). *The Message* says, *"Humans are satisfied with whatever looks good; God probes for what is good."* There is a double accountability for the Christian leader. She needs to meet the standards of her particular assignment, but there is a higher accountability to God and His standards.

A woman striving for balance in any leadership role needs to be **visionary.** This word really isn't as scary as it sounds, although it does involve several different things that are of tremendous importance. Any leader enlisted, elected, or called to perform a prescribed list of responsibilities will need to be a visionary. A leader without vision will not have many followers, and if she does by chance, they won't stay long! Being a visionary calls for a specific way of thinking. Not every leader is brilliant, nor does she walk around with her head in a cloud. To be a visionary means that a woman has the ability to look into the future—not to see what is going to happen, but to anticipate what needs to happen. A futurist (visionary) is not synonymous with a fortune-teller! It doesn't mean that you as a leader have all the answers and can solve all the problems. It simply means that you are able to use your imagination to look at things from a different perspective, perhaps more creatively than other people. If you truly desire to be a woman who has balance in her approach to leadership, you need to be visionary in your outlook.

Last, a real leader is one who **develops other leaders**. John C. Maxwell, author of *Developing the Leader Within You*, believes that a great deal of a leader's time should be spent enlisting, equipping, training, and mentoring future leaders. It will be of little value when you look back on your years of leadership to see that what you accomplished all but faded away because you were no longer there. Developing new leaders is another staple, like the potato, for the implementation of sound strategies, good plans, and innovative ideas. As women assume leadership positions in the workplace, in local community government, in education, in their families, and within their churches, they will continue to see the need of achieving balance in what they do. That balance in part will be determined by their ability to develop other leaders. The future of our families, churches, communities, and other organizations depends on it.

Accomplishment, achievement, and notoriety are not what make us effective leaders. Our approach to leadership cannot be driven by a desire for power or influence, but rather by a desire to help others and to meet their needs. How we strive to meet those needs will demonstrate what kind of servant leaders we are.

Integrity is critical to our effectiveness as a leader in any position. We must be women whose word means something, women whose character and behavior are Christ-like, and women who are honest in relationships with others. We must have a servant approach to what we do as we fulfill our duties and carry out the tasks assigned to us. Accountability is at the very foundation of any leadership role we may assume. Our commitment to hard work and dependability will set us apart as leaders who are interested in maintaining quality and reliability.

Being a visionary is not always easy. Not everyone understands the drive a leader has to push forward, to strive for the next goal. However, vision must be in place in every organization or it will have no future. A woman working toward creating a balance in her leadership efforts needs to be a visionary—always looking ahead, thinking outside of the box, and searching for new points of view.

Developing new leaders is not an easy task, and so, it is often put on the bottom of a leader's to-do list. Isn't it easier just to do it yourself? Of course it usually is. Investing your life and time (lots of time) in someone else who may not have the same abilities or outlook is hard to do. It requires a lot of effort and can result in less-than-perfect outcomes. The project may not be done the way *you* wanted it done. However, doing everything ourselves is not a healthy option. The job gets done, yes. But no one learned how to do anything. No one new was involved. No one was equipped for the future of the organization.

In summary then, we must first build our lives on Jesus. He is the foundation or staple, if you will. From that essential basis our lives can flourish, and we can grow in fruitful, balanced leadership remembering the five basic ingredients of integrity, servant outlook, accountability, vision, and the ability to develop other leaders. Each element should be present in our lives as we try to be the kind of leaders that are not only effective but pleasing to God.

Equipoise—Max De Pree in *Leadership Jazz* says, "Leadership can never stop at words. Leaders must act and they do so only in the context of their beliefs." If women want to be effective leaders and have balance in their lives, they must begin with a commitment to God and His precepts. Having a personal relationship with Jesus is the only way to begin walking with God and seeking His will in all of life's situations. Balance in a leader's life must begin with a salvation experience.

God's Symmetry—*[W]e are saved because the Master Jesus amazingly and out of sheer generosity moved to save us.*
—Acts 15:11

Tipping the Scales—Set a timer for ten minutes and use that time to write down how your relationship with Jesus has made a difference in your life as a leader.

Notes

Prayerfully review the chapter.

What is God calling you to do?

How can the lessons of this chapter help you become a better leader?

What steps do you need to take next?

Nailing It Down

◇◇◇◇◇◇◇◇

Keep your eyes open,
hold tight to your convictions,
give it all you've got, be resolute.
—1 Corinthians 16:13

◇◇◇◇◇◇◇◇

A woman's convictions are an important part of her life. If a woman doesn't know what she believes or gives no thought to where she "draws the line," she will never be as effective a witness as she can be. Not only will her personal life suffer, but as a leader, she will not be as confident and successful as she could otherwise be. If a woman does not establish any boundaries, she will continually revisit decisions that could have been already made had she determined what her beliefs were ahead of time. Making decisions over and over again takes time and energy. Nail them down!

For this chapter, let's use nails to symbolize the convictions women need to have in their lives. Years ago, it was popular in many churches to write in the front of a person's Bible the date of his or her salvation experience. It was called "nailing it down" and served to remind the person of what had happened in his/her heart that special day. If women are to live abundant lives, they must establish what their core ideology is, in other words, what their convictions are.

Here's an example of *not* having your convictions "nailed down" and how that can undermine your effectiveness for God. Years ago my husband and I taught a coed Bible study group of adults in their 40s. Several Sundays went by and one man and his wife were absent. When we contacted them, his response was, "Well, you know, when Sunday morning comes, I have to decide whether I will attend church that day." My husband's response to him was that an active Christian should already have made that decision. He told the man that a decision to attend church shouldn't have to be made over and over again. The truth of the matter was that the man didn't have a conviction about regular church attendance.

A wise friend of mine once said, "I have chosen a certain Bible verse as my life verse. It is my heart's conviction about how I will live my life. It serves as a filter for every decision I make and everything I do." What a tremendous way to live your life.

▬ Biblical Snapshot ▬

The story of Naaman, a general in the Syrian army, is recorded in 2 Kings 5:1–19. At some point, his army had gone out of Syria into Israel and had brought back captives. One of those captives, a young girl, became a personal slave to Naaman's wife. A victim of war carried away to a foreign country, she was a slave in the household of a powerful man. Very little is known about the young girl. Even though she had not reached maturity, her actions show her to be wise beyond her years.

Naaman is described as a *"man of valor"* but the verse continues, *"but he was a leper"* (2 Kings 5:1 AMP). All of his accomplishments, power, wealth, and prestige were set aside as if they meant nothing in the dilemma of being a leper. Leprosy has always been a dreaded disease. Lepers were literally outcasts from society, forced to live in caves, and left to a life of begging. For hundreds of years all forms of the disease were believed to be contagious, so families in despair abandoned their loved ones for fear of catching leprosy. Only wealth and power prevented that from happening to Naaman.

Even though everything had been taken away from the slave girl, her trust in God had not been tainted or diminished. 2 Kings 5:3 shows her concern for her master and his predicament, *"Would that my lord were with the prophet that is in Samaria!"* (AMP). She could have hated Naaman, but instead she was concerned about him. Her conviction that God was all-powerful and faithful enabled

---

her to speak up and suggest that Naaman present himself to the prophet Elisha.

Naaman traveled to Samaria to see Elisha and was angered because Elisha sent out a servant to tell him what to do rather than seeing him himself. As if that wasn't enough of an insult, his instructions were to dip himself seven times in the Jordan River. By Naaman's standards this was unthinkable, so at first he refused to do so. Talked into following Elisha's secondhand directions, Naaman went to the Jordan, dipped himself the prescribed number of times, and was healed of his leprosy. The statement Jesus makes years later could not have been made except for the convictions of a young slave girl. *"There were many lepers in Israel in the time of Elisha the prophet, and yet not one of them was cleansed (by being healed), but only Naaman the Syrian"* (Luke 4:27 AMP). It is doubtful that we would have heard about Naaman again had she not been convicted that God could heal him.

In reflecting about this slave girl, in light of the changes in our society, it would be easy to dismiss what she did as "nothing too special." For a slave to suggest anything could put her life in jeopardy. She had absolutely no standing in Naaman's household and was of no consequence whatsoever. She was a child, a slave, and a female. Torn away from her family, she was alone and most likely mourning all her losses. Her early training at her mother's feet perhaps taught her that God was the true healer, and that faith caused her to look beyond her immediate circumstances and live out her convictions. She had positive news and was determined to share it! She knew something that was right and true and wanted her master to reap the benefits of that knowledge. A person may seem to be, or may regard herself to be insignificant, but when she stands firm in her convictions, history can be changed and lives transformed.

Because of the various home improvement projects my husband and I have done together, I can identify several types of nails. When we reroofed one of our houses (no, I wasn't on the roof—I prepared snacks down below!), I found roofing nails all over the house—in the washing machine, on the floor, in pockets, embedded in the carpet. I know roofing nails have little ridges and are usually grey with a wide head. Nailing baseboards requires finishing nails, which are slim with small heads requiring a "sinker" to countersink them into the wood for filling with wood putty later. Drywall nails are found in another bin at the home improvement store. They are black and narrow with a wide head. The shaft has ridges to help anchor the drywall to the studs. Each kind of nail serves a specific purpose and will help the user complete a project with success.

The various types of nails are not unlike the different categories of convictions we hold that relate to our daily lives.

1. Marriage

One category involves marriage. When a woman marries, she makes a commitment to keep her marriage vows. She needs to have convictions about the sanctity of marriage and that she will abide by biblical standards for the relationship between a man and a woman. Her convictions about the marriage relationship won't make her immune to temptations, but she will have a filter in place to help her remain faithful to her vows. The best time for a woman to decide on her convictions about the marriage relationship is before the wedding takes place. Convictions about how a man and woman will treat one another, how they will solve their differences, how crises will be handled, and how they will honor God in their home come out of concentrated time spent together with God in prayer and Bible study. Psalm 127:1 puts all of this into perspective, *"Except the Lord build the house, they labor in vain that build it"* (KJV).

2. Parenting

A mother must have some convictions about how children should be reared. Isn't it a lot easier just to go along with that teenager who wants to do something "just this once?" If there are standards, God's standards, in place when children ask those difficult "why" questions, you will have a ready answer, an answer that has been formed from studying God's Word. You will be able to explain how God led you to a specific conviction and how He has helped you understand what to do.

Years ago when our only daughter was a young teenager, she made plans to go to a movie with friends. It was our conviction as parents that our children would not be allowed to see movies with a rating higher than PG. On this particular night, her father transported her to the movie theater to meet her friends. When they arrived, he asked which movie she was seeing. There on the marquee was the rating, "PG–13." Now, our daughter had called the theater for the rating and the recording listed it as "PG."

Obviously, something was amiss! She went to the ticket window to confirm the rating and returned to the car with tears in her eyes. PG–13 was the correct rating but couldn't she see just this one? A semi-heated discussion followed, but dad's conviction held, and the two of them drove home in silence.

It would have been much easier to give in and allow our daughter to see "just one," but we couldn't do that. We kept the conviction God had led us to make. As I observe our daughter's young family today I see some of the same convictions in place that we had while our three children were growing up. By living out their convictions she and her husband are *"providing a circle of quiet within the clamor of evil"* (Psalm 94:12) as they rear their three little ones.

3. In the Workplace

The media is full of accounts of women (and men) who have made decisions to disregard the rights of others to further their own agendas. The workplace today is not an easy place for an individual who has Christian convictions. Unethical practices are rampant, and Christian women must, sometimes on a daily basis, make the decision whether to succumb to the pressure to conform, or just "go along." The pressure is sometimes so intense that it becomes a choice between keeping the job, advancing in a career, or leaving the position. Decisions like these are difficult ones to make when financial issues are pressing in. Needless to say, we agree they are unfair. But they should come as no surprise to any of us, because we are warned in the Bible that we will face scrutiny and even hostility from others when we stand up for what we believe to be right and moral. We are told, *"Keep vigilant watch over your heart . . . keep your eyes straight ahead; ignore all sideshow distractions. Watch your step . . . looking neither right nor left"* (Proverbs 4:23–27).

As the number of women in the workplace has increased over the years, their influence on corporate culture has also increased. Women have brought a "softening" and a nurturing aspect into corporations and businesses. Their presence has created new kinds of networking and enabled excellent teamwork efforts. What they have added, however, has in no way made them exempt from having to face the discomfort of being the only voice raised in defense of an injustice or from being the only one to not participate in an ungodly activity. Just as Christian men have faced this dilemma, it is now something that happens frequently to women as they strive for advancement in the workplace. Having convictions frees a person from having to make decisions over and over in each situation.

4. Crisis Situations

The Bible contains many illustrations of how God's people dealt with crisis when it came into their lives. The convictions that guided them became obvious. When God asked Abraham to leave his fatherland, Abraham acted on faith, living out his conviction that God would always be with him. That enabled him to leave everything he knew to follow God. Likewise, the convictions of Shadrach, Meshach, and Abednego were made public when they were cast into a furnace for refusing to bow down before the king as a god. Later, Daniel was thrown into a pit of lions because of his convictions. His life was spared and *"no hurt of any kind was found on him, because he believed in (relied on, adhered to, and trusted in)—his God"* (Daniel 6:23 AMP). Esther's faithfulness and willingness to put her life on the line and stand against injustice serves as an example to us. Her story demonstrates how God will intervene and protect His people.

What could happen if each of us, in our own spheres of influence, were to stand up and be counted for what is morally and ethically right? Would we make an impact on our world today? Would our cities be changed? Would lives be transformed, families restored?

A director of a volunteer worldwide missions program told the story of meeting with two young women who came to him during volunteer training. They asked him to specifically train them to become martyrs for Christ because that is what they felt might be asked of them, and they wanted to be prepared. I daresay that not many of us have this attitude when we approach crisis situations in our lives. We are interested in extricating ourselves with minimal damage to our lifestyles, schedules, and prospects.

Just as there are numerous nails all designed with a specific purpose in mind, there are many categories or sections of life that require us to develop a conviction about what is right and wrong. Marriage, parenting, working with others, and crisis situations demand our response. How much easier life is for us when we simply stand on the convictions we have formed from our daily walk with God through Bible study and prayer! Will stressful situations disappear from our marriages, families, workplace, or church life? Of course not, but we can be assured from God's Word that *"The path of right-living people is level. The Leveler evens the road for the right-living"* (Isaiah 26:7).

No Shortcuts

In my experience (which granted, is limited) nails serve a very important function in almost all home improvement projects. I'll have to admit that there may be more nails than necessary in some things I have nailed but the board stayed in place! A number of years ago I had the opportunity to participate in a house-building blitz sponsored by Habitat for Humanity and a women's organization. I chose to work on a house in Portland, Oregon. (The alternative was New Mexico in July. I think not!) Because the house plans were drawn for a dwelling on an irregularly shaped lot, a lot of the labor exceeded our very low level of expertise. But, we *could* nail four-by-eight-foot sheets of plywood in place in preparation for the siding. I'd never nailed as many nails as I did in those three days! We used nails designed for the work we were doing. Finishing nails would not have done the job. Roofing nails would have been too short. My point in this nail story is this: there is a purpose for each kind of nail. There is a purpose for the convictions we are to develop too.

The wisdom found in Proverbs sums it all up, *"A thick bankroll is no help when life falls apart, but a principled life can stand up to the worst"* (Proverbs 11:4). God intends for His people to live their lives to the fullest because He has given us so much. It makes perfect sense that we learn all we can about His precepts. Every standard God gives us is for a specific purpose. He has a guideline for every situation even though it may not be stated in today's terminology. The concept is there for us to find with the guidance of the Holy Spirit. The Bible is, in fact, a *"lamp unto* [our] *feet and a light unto* [our] *path"* (Psalm 119:105 KJV). When we have done our part in discovering how God wants us to behave, relate to others, make decisions, rear our children, function in His church, and develop that knowledge into a system of convictions, our lives will be blessed and rewarding. Each discovery we make, every "ah-ha" moment we have, will serve to make us more aware of God's presence in our daily lives and in all that we do.

As we search for balance in our lives, it is easy to get caught up in all the demands of daily life. The search for balance, which is what God wants for us, becomes lost in the details of life itself. Our beliefs must be founded in God's Word and lived out with His hand on us. The decisions we make, the paths we choose, and the choices we make will be reflections of those beliefs. There are no shortcuts to well-defined, God-led convictions.

Before reading any further, stop here and think about how your convictions affect your leadership roles.

- Reflect on a time at work when you explained your conviction about something that was contrary to the prevailing attitude or idea.

- Search out one Scripture verse that has helped you regarding moral behavior in your marriage or another relationship.

- How has Jesus's example of moral leadership helped you in a leadership role?

- Write down one conviction you have regarding the four areas discussed previously in this chapter.

A popular television show on the Food Network features all the shortcuts you can take to produce home-cooked meals in record time. Precut, preshredded, precooked food can make the cook's life much easier. Microwaves can make mac 'n cheese in a flash, heat soup, and even bake brownies in a fraction of the time it would take to boil water and heat up an oven. We love instant stuff and shortcuts!

While these shortcuts help us manage our time, there are no shortcuts in the preparation of a leader. Developing an understanding of God's Word and its application to us does not happen overnight. The same is true regarding a woman in her development as a leader. Those of us in leadership positions must be observant of another woman's convictions before we enlist her to accept a leadership role. We know that a person will bring along her own convictions. The wrong person for the job may cause a project to fail. Anyone who operates under the conviction that she is the only one who matters, that she is above any rule or regulation, does not have leadership potential.

"Leadership doesn't begin with techniques but with premises, not with tools, but with beliefs, not with systems but with understandings," says leadership specialist, Max De Pree in *Leadership Jazz*. Techniques are certainly a part of any woman's leadership skill set, as are the tools she has to use. She needs knowledge of systems, processes, and how things work, but none of these things can take the place of principles, beliefs, and understanding.

Leading with Conviction
What, then, does a woman who leads with conviction look like?

Circle the words that describe you.

> tall, short, overweight, thin, glasses, contact lenses, curly hair, short hair, mature, young, wearing a suit, dressed in jeans, retired, with preschoolers in tow, carrying a briefcase or laptop computer, holding a sack of groceries, wearing a backpack, holding a baby, wearing gardening gloves, reading a book

How did you describe yourself? Did you circle more than three words? Women are multidimensional, so more than one word or phrase will be used to paint an image of what you look like. The words used to describe you may not be the same ones that create a visual picture of someone else. And that's OK! Just as we don't look or think alike, we lead in different ways and when observers look at us, they see different aspects of character.

When we lead, people must decide if they are going to follow us. Did you know that if no one is following you, you aren't leading? What causes people to follow someone? Do the majority of individuals demand something of their leaders? Let's try to answer some questions about how a woman leads out of her convictions.

1. *Should a woman lead from a conviction that God wants her to be prepared as a leader?*
There is a passage in Proverbs 2:9–15 that is especially meaningful in relation to leading with conviction. When we accept the call to leadership, regardless of the kind of role it is, God wants to be at the center. The decisions we make and the directions we take as leaders can create confusion and disharmony, or they can glorify God and

help create better organizations. This particular passage speaks about a leader needing to seek Lady Wisdom, Brother Knowledge, and Good Sense. That means being prepared. Being prepared prevents our taking advice and directions from others who are lost and confused themselves. The writer of *The Message* describes these people this way: *"they can't tell a trail from a tumbleweed"* (verse 15). All too often, when we begin a leadership journey we ask the wrong people for directions and advice. That's when we get into trouble. Preparation is critical for a woman desiring to lead out of a conviction that God wants her best effort.

Preparing oneself for leading comes in many forms. To lead a Bible study requires preparation by studying God's Word, using commentaries, and reading other resources. Preparing to lead seminars on specific topics should begin with basic conference-leading techniques. This training can be received by attending local, regional, state, and even national events that are designed to equip women to be effective leaders.

A leadership position in the workplace may require a person to take seminars and workshops. Even community leadership roles demand a person to attend information and procedure sessions to equip her with key skills necessary for the job. Regardless of the kind of leadership role a woman is asked to assume, preparation is a vital element. If a woman is to lead from her convictions, she needs to be certain she has determined how she will face opposition, unethical behavior, and unhealthy situations *before* she accepts the position. Having made a commitment about her Christian witness ahead of time will make future decision making easier. Then, she can agree with Paul's admonition, *"Whatever you have learned* or received, or heard from me, or seen in me—put it into practice" (Philippians 4:9 TNIV).

Frances Hesselbein, former CEO of the Girl Scouts of America, notes, "the longest lasting organizations are usually blessed with leaders who have a sense of ethics and personal integrity" (from *Leadership Secrets from the Bible* by Lorin Woolfe). Women must prepare for their leadership roles and work from their conviction about the value of that *preparation*.

2. *Is a conviction about being morally upright and above reproach important to a woman in leadership?*

In a society that touts tolerance as more desirable than anything else, Christian women in the workplace are often regarded as being "behind the times," "prudes," or religious fanatics. What course of action do Christian women need to be prepared to take? What kind of boundaries do they need to have in order to survive the workplace and continue with God's approval? Obviously, there are many questions related to this area and it seems as if there are no easy answers. We know that God tries our hearts and is *"pleased with integrity"* (1 Chronicles 29:17 TNIV). A leader's integrity or lack of it becomes evident in times of crisis. Therefore, a woman must test her convictions against what God says in His Word.

Compromise often follows closely behind the world's concept of tolerance. Society would have us find the middle ground, participate in the "give and take," in every situation. What is the result of doing this? Compromise. And compromise can be destructive. Christian women in leadership positions need to be known not for their compromises but for their convictions. Ephesians 6:14–18 (AMP) is a familiar passage that speaks to developing a moral compass about right and wrong. Phrases such as *"hold your ground," "keep alert,"* and *"watch with strong purpose"* call us as believers to lead with conviction that God's principles are sound and true even in today's "enlightened" world.

A woman who wants to lead with balance in her life will lead from convictions about what constitutes ethical behavior, what is just, and how God's name can be lifted up in each situation. Leading in her home will require decisions about right and wrong, parenting, and her marriage relationship. Leading in her neighborhood may mean she has to take a stand against prejudice and the way some persons are treated. Leading at work might involve objecting to sexual innuendos or harassment. Assuming a leadership role in her church could mean speaking up about the way money is used. Any leadership position will require on-the-spot decisions regarding process, purpose, and direction. A prepared woman will make those decisions based on her convictions about what is right and morally acceptable in God's eyes.

3. *How does knowledge play a role in developing convictions for balanced leading?*

God intends for us to learn. The writer of Proverbs says that knowledge is pleasant (see Proverbs 2:10) and that the fear of God is the beginning of knowledge (see Proverbs 1:7). The psalmist asks God for good judgment (see Psalm 119:66). Wanting to learn and being curious are healthy aspects of leadership development.

Knowledge of what a leadership role involves and what the responsibilities are is a basic beginning point for a leader. Knowledge does not end with the acquisition of skills and information gleaned from books however.

Any leadership role involves human beings, so "people skills" are necessary. This is not knowledge that comes naturally to some women. You should want to lead from the conviction that God loves everyone and that every individual has worth. This will assure that your leadership approach holds that same value.

Remember, there are no shortcuts to developing as a leader. While you may be able to take a crash course in computer programming and jump right into a new job, the same is not true for making your convictions an integral part of your leadership approach. It takes patience and persistence to reach the point where your knowledge works out of your convictions.

For *Women, Faith, and Work*, Lois Flowers also interviewed Pin Pin Chau, a bank CEO in Atlanta. Chau said, "In the 12 years I've been CEO, I have found that if I act out of conviction, after prayerful consideration, then I can sit and wait for God to vindicate me. I get my strength through knowing His word and knowing that His unfailing love will always be there for me. It will not be shaken."

4. *What does confidence have to do with leading from your convictions?*

We are made in whose image? Do we really believe we are to be instruments in God's hands? The psalmist says that we are marvelously made (see Psalm 139:14). We as women can lead with confidence, because of the conviction that we are made in God's image and that He has gifted us with abilities, insights, and personalities. God's Word tells us He has a plan for us and that the plan is for our good (see Jeremiah 29:11). We lead with confidence that grows from knowledge and preparation. Our confidence for the tasks of leadership comes from the conviction that God has put His hand on us and has given us the potential to do what He asks us to do.

When women look in the mirror, they see many things! They may see someone who is too fat, too skinny, too old, too grey, too many wrinkles, and on the list goes. All too often we see only our deficiencies and not the special abilities that God sees. M. Scott Peck, put it wisely, "Until you value yourself you will not value your time. Until you value your time, you will not do anything with it" (quoted in *Checklist for Life for Leaders*).

- Read the following Scripture passages to help you understand that God values you and that you can have confidence to do what He gives you opportunity to do: Genesis 1:27; Matthew 10:29–31; Romans 8:17; Psalm 139; 2 Corinthians 4:7.

- Memorize 1 John 3:1. Confide to a friend the self-esteem issue you struggle with the most and enlist her as your prayer partner.

A woman of conviction realizes that preparation and knowledge are necessary to carry out the responsibilities of her leadership role, and she can be confident leading from what she believes to be morally right.

5. *How do a woman's convictions about relationships influence how she leads?*
"*Love and truth form a good leader; sound leadership is founded on loving integrity*" (Proverbs 20:28). If a leader treats the people around her like they are there simply to do her bidding, to be used for her purposes, or to attract attention to her, she is displaying the conviction that she

is the only important person and others are to be used. On the other hand, the leader who respects and values the people around her demonstrates loving integrity. Scripture instructs us to love each other and to seek peace with all people (Hebrews 13:1; 12:14). If this is a woman's conviction, it will be to her advantage as a leader to develop good people skills.

Your people skills will not only demonstrate that you have the expertise (knowledge) to do the job but that you value others' contributions to the activity or project as well. For several years, I lived in a mobile home park. The park manager and her husband were not the most approachable people I've met. It seemed as if they were at a complete loss as to how to relate to others. Even though they had owned the park since its beginning, they were virtually clueless about carrying on a conversation or dealing with people in a friendly, cordial manner. The basket of Christmas goodies I delivered to them the first year we were there was met with blank looks and the woman said, "Why would you do this?"

Leadership is not all about the task, nor is it about your ability to coordinate the work. Most of the time success hinges on your ability to develop followers who are convinced where you are leading is the direction they want to take.

Taking Stock

Take a quick people-skills test. Rate yourself on a scale of 1 to 5, with 5 being the highest.

- Do you treat others with respect and dignity?
- Do you practice acts of kindness every day?

- Does the way you lead indicate that you realize your actions mean more than what you say?
- Do you appreciate the talents and abilities of those under your leadership?
- Do you actually love people?

Out of a possible score of 25 if your answers total 21–25, consider yourself to be in balance as your convictions influence your attitude about people. If your total is 16–20, you are doing fairly well in creating healthy relationships with your followers. If your score falls between 10–15, you need to intentionally address these areas. If the total is under 10, read Proverbs 18:24, John 15:13, and Hosea 11:4 to see how you can be better balanced in your people skills.

Without people, an organization will lose its purpose and value and cease to exist. As a female leader, your beliefs about the value of human beings and their worth to God will be displayed for all to see even though you may not intend for that to happen. John C. Maxwell in his book *Developing the Leader Within You* says, "Who we are determines what we do." You cannot say one thing and do another by your actions.

The woman whose leadership approach is based on her convictions will be prepared, morally upright, knowledgeable, confident, and relate well to others out of love.

It is true that not every woman who can make a difference is willing to make a difference. Determine today, that with God's help, you will be an effective, balanced leader leading from your convictions.

Equipoise—Conviction is defined as a belief or principle. A Christian woman leading in any area of her life must base her beliefs on what she has discovered in the Bible. Opinion, on the other hand, is an attitude or outlook that may or may not be biblically based. Many times, it is *our* thought rather than something inspired by God.

God's Symmetry—*His delight and desire are in the law of the Lord, and on His law he habitually meditates by day and by night.*
—Psalm 1:2

Tipping the Scales—Ask someone whose convictions you admire what they do to foster good relationships with their followers.

Notes

Prayerfully review the chapter.

What is God calling you to do?

How can the lessons of this chapter help you become a better leader?

What steps do you need to take next?

3

Laughter Is the Best Medicine

◇◇◇◇◇◇◇◇

He will yet fill your mouth with laughing,
and your lips with rejoicing.
—Job 8:21 (NKJV)

◇◇◇◇◇◇◇◇

id you hear the one about…? Prisoners in isolation shared jokes back and forth by calling out numbers that had been assigned to the old jokes they told. One prisoner called out "39," and everyone laughed heartily. Another yelled "27" and again, everyone laughed like it was the funniest joke they had ever heard. Not to be left out, one new prisoner called "17" but there was no laughter. He tried again, "54." Still no response. "What's the matter?" he asked. "Some people just can't tell a joke," came the reply.

As we come to laughter and humor and the part it should play in every woman's life, set out a bowl of nuts to remind you that a sense of humor is critical for Christ followers. The saying "If you don't laugh, you'll go nuts" explains why I chose nuts to represent humor, which is critical to keep a woman's life enjoyable and manageable. Mark Twain said we ought to live our lives in such a way that even the undertaker is sad when we die!

Sadness, tragedy, and trials come into every woman's life, so we must work hard at keeping a positive perspective. Look in a mirror and think about what you see. Do you see a woman with furrowed brow, grimace lines around her eyes, and her mouth in a tight, thin line? Ruth Senter, in her book *Have We Really Come A Long Way?*, suggests that while it is true that women have made great strides in equal pay for equal work and are now able to enter almost every profession, they have perhaps done some trading not to their advantage. She believes that many women in their search for "everything" have sacrificed optimism and cheerfulness. She believes that women have lost joy in their lives.

Years ago, I had a friend whose birthday was early in the year when skies were gloomy, and the weather was below freezing. My friend lost her ability to laugh about this time of year as her birthday reminded her too much of the passing of time. I started making January survival kits for her birthday gifts. Every year I gathered cheerful items including crossword puzzle books, a mug and tea bags, a paperback mystery, candy bars, and the like. The gift was always well received, and for a few days at least, the joy in living returned in spite of the overcast skies.

> *Laughter is like changing a baby's diaper—it doesn't solve any problems permanently but it makes things more acceptable for a while.*

The grey skies will come, uncertainty brought on by despair will surface, and any thought of laughter and joy seemingly will be left behind. These are the times when we need to remember the importance of laughter and joy—the prescription to lift our spirits. *"A cheerful heart is good medicine, but a crushed spirit dries up the bones"* (Proverbs 17:22 TNIV).

Did you know that laughter is actually attributed to God on three occasions? In Psalm 37:13 David writes that when the wicked devise plots against the righteous man, the Lord laughs *"for He sees that their own day of defeat is coming"* (AMP). When King Saul sent men to watch David's house for a chance to kill him, David calls out to God for deliverance from his enemies. He acknowledges, *"You, O Lord, will laugh at them in scorn"* (Psalm 59:8 AMP). The writer of Proverbs records that if the scoffers who hate Wisdom will repent, then God will pour out His spirit upon them. They don't do that so God says, *"I also will laugh at your calamity"* (Proverbs 1:26 AMP).

Abraham's wife, Sarah, is the only Bible character recorded to have laughed, *"God has made me to laugh; all who hear will laugh with me"* (Genesis 21:6 AMP). What one of us if we were told we would become pregnant at age 90 wouldn't have laughed?

Because God's Word is without error and speaks to every need we will ever have, it should not surprise us that scientists have discovered medical benefits to laughter.

Diet definition: A short period of starvation preceding a gain of five pounds.

Laughter is thought to alleviate hypertension, arthritis, and migraines. It lowers blood pressure, reduces stress hormones, and boosts immune functions. This happens because as laughter exercises various body muscles, it triggers the release of endorphins, the body's natural painkillers. Read the list below to see how laughter has a positive effect on your body!

- Carbon dioxide is driven out of your body and replaced by oxygen-rich air, giving you physical and mental freshness.
- Laughter can produce anti-inflammatory agents that might aid in back pain.
- Muscles are encouraged to relax when you laugh.
- Laughter exercises facial muscles to prevent aging.
- Anger can be dissolved by laughing.
- Laughter is a mood elevator and fosters immediate relaxation.
- Your diaphragm, abdominal, back, face, and leg muscles are all exercised. (It has been likened to stationary jogging or internal aerobics.)

Not only does laughter benefit us physically, it also carries social benefits as well. Laughter is the shortest distance between two people, and serves as a connector. It can heal misunderstandings, or at least serve as a meeting ground for discussion. Laughter is enjoyed best when it is shared, and has an excellent way of teaching us perspective.

If laughter can bring all these benefits into our lives, why in the world don't we laugh more? I don't know about you, but I like that part about laughter reducing facial aging. And what about the exercise? That sounds like my kind of exercise!

A sense of humor definitely helps as financial pressures increase, marital differences appear, or assignments at work become too heavy. Women are more likely to thrive if they interject laughter into their days and work on developing a better sense of humor. Allen Klein, who lectures on healing through humor, claims that children laugh 400 times a day while adults laugh only 15 times a day (source: http://blog.christianitytoday.com/buildingadultministries/2008/09/everlaughing_life.html). Recognizing that adults deal with serious issues and that life is often less than pleasant, it would be a step in the right direction to practice laughing more!

You know it's going to be a bad day when your four-year-old tells you it's almost impossible to flush a grapefruit.

▬ Biblical Snapshot ▬

When life takes a turn for the worse, when relationships are rocky, work isn't going well, the neighbors are complaining about your kids, the pastor doesn't like your women's retreat plans, or your husband forgot your wedding anniversary, where is the joy? Forget the laughter, the sense of humor—isn't there any joy? The Bible has a lot to say about joy.

While laughter is often just an outward sign and may not be a true indication of an inner joy, such joy is possible because God is all about giving us joy. When thinking about joy, three women in the Bible come to mind because of their life situations and how they responded to God's guidance in their lives.

Deborah—Deborah was the only female judge selected by God to lead the people of Israel at a time in their history when they had—again—stopped following God. They had a pattern of following God for a while and then moving away from Him to do what they wanted to do. Trouble would follow that decision, and they would cry out to God for mercy asking Him to save them—again. Deborah was a judge who settled disputes for Israel. She was also the one God chose to free His people from the domination of the Canaanites. The Canaanites were particularly cruel and had oppressed the Israelites for 20 years. God told Deborah that Barak was to lead the Israelites to fight the Canaanites, and He would give them a victory. When Deborah relayed this message to Barak, he replied that the only way he would go into battle was if she would go with him. She agreed but cautioned him that he would receive no credit for winning the battle because of his cowardice.

The Israelites did win the battle and the Canaanite general, Sisera, was killed. God's people were free once more to worship Him and live under His merciful watch-care. While the song recorded in Judges 5 is basically a song of victory, Deborah's joy is evident as she praises God. *"I, even I, will sing unto the LORD; I will sing praise to* the LORD God of Israel" (Judges 5:3 KJV). Read the entire account in your Bible and notice Deborah's excitement as she records the events of battle. More importantly, reading between the lines will give you a vivid picture of a woman who has let God use her for great things. He used her willingness and her abilities to accomplish His will. Watching God work is an amazing thing and brings great joy.

Deborah provides us with an example of a woman whose life had been turned upside down by change. We don't have any information about her life prior to being selected by God to be Israel's judge. Regardless of the ways she spent her days, becoming a judge changed everything. Needless to say, going into battle was not one of her life goals or a part of her plans. However, Deborah was willing to help Barak work through his fear of leading Israel into battle. Her life took an unexpected turn, but she was still able to express joy at what God accomplished through her. It wouldn't be difficult to imagine Deborah laughing at the adventures she had!

Hannah—The story of Hannah, one of Elkanah's two wives, is told in 1 Samuel. We know that Elkanah loved Hannah because he gave her a generous portion at the sacrificial meal because *"he loved her"* (1Samuel 1:5). Nevertheless, Hannah, through no wrongdoing of her own, was on the outside of society. Elkanah's other wife never let Hannah forget that she had failed miserably, because she had not given Elkanah any children. A woman in Jewish society who did not bear children was considered incomplete and flawed. Because of her great sorrow and the constant haranguing of the other wife, Hannah was miserable. As the family traveled to observe the religious rituals, she would always pray that

God would give her a child. She was so intent on her prayers and so miserable that Elkanah noticed she was in tears. But then, when she was in the Temple, Eli, the priest, noticed her praying. Thinking she was drunk, he rebuked her. But, when he found out what was wrong, he said, *"Go in peace. And may the God of Israel give you what you have asked of him"* (1 Samuel 1:17).

Hannah left the Temple and the Scripture says her face was radiant. You know the rest of the story. Hannah gave birth to a baby boy the next year, and she named him Samuel, which means "heard of God." Her entire life changed because of God's faithfulness to answer her prayers for a child. Her song of praise is recorded in the second chapter of 1 Samuel. She thanks God for His salvation, His protection, and His deliverance. Out of the depths of despair, Hannah emerged as a woman full of joy and gratitude for what had happened in her life. Would she have still been faithful had God not answered her prayers as He did? Or did He answer the prayers because of her faithfulness to Him through the years? Regardless of how you answer, Hannah's joy is unmistakable as she sings, *"There is none holy like the Lord; there is no Rock like our God"* (1 Samuel 2:2 AMP).

Mary—Mary is a frequent subject for study among women. Her story has been told and retold through the centuries. Nonetheless very little is known about Mary. Scripture simply describes her as a young virgin engaged to a descendant of David. Portraits by master painters present her as an attractive young woman with a hint of mystery. Whether she was pretty, homely, tall, or short is not really an issue. We wonder what her personality was like—was she energetic, outgoing, personable? However, her personality traits don't constitute a major concern either.

Now her character...that's another matter. Was she perfect? Of course not. Only her Son is perfect and worthy of worship. But it is inconceivable to me that God would choose a woman to bear His Son who did not exhibit integrity, concern for others, stability, strength, and grace.

When the angel Gabriel went to Nazareth to visit Mary, he brought her disturbing news. Imagine what she must have thought when he called her "favored one" and told her she was "blessed before all other women!" The greeting may have confused Mary, but Gabriel's next words made her head spin. Hearing that she would conceive a child and that the child would be called the Son of the Most High would concern anyone.

Jews of that day were looking for Messiah as evidenced by Anna and Simeon in the Temple (Luke 2:21–38). The amazing thing was that God had chosen Mary. We see nothing in Scripture that indicates Mary tried to refuse the honor or that she responded negatively to what Gabriel told her. In fact, she set aside any control she might have had and said, *"Let it be with me just as you say"* (Luke 1:38). When the angel left, Mary went to visit her cousin Elizabeth in Judah. Elizabeth realized immediately that something had happened to Mary. Mary sang her response to Elizabeth. Read Luke 1:46–55 aloud and listen for the joy that permeates the song. Her words ring out as if she cannot contain them any longer.

Mary probably had many thoughts and questions swirling in her mind. What would her village say? What would Joseph do about their engagement and coming wedding? In the days ahead there would be more questions and other uncertainties, but Mary could rejoice in her situation, because she was secure in the knowledge that God was in control. She experienced pure, undiluted joy even in the face of scrutiny and gossip. While to the observer's eye, her life was in shambles, she rested on God's mercy and relied on His grace. Joy put balance back in her life.

Leading with Humor

To summarize this chapter so far: looking for humor in life's circumstances can be the difference between sanity and total desperation. If your bowl of nuts isn't within easy reach or full enough, you may need to pull it closer or refill it. If you haven't needed it today to remind you that you need to balance your life with humor, you'll need it soon—maybe tomorrow!

Understandably, if our personal lives require us to have a sense of humor then as leaders it becomes even more important. As women in leadership positions, we must develop a sense of humor to enable us to work with team members, subordinates, community leaders, and those difficult people with whom we come in contact. In an article he wrote for *Forbes Magazine* Paul Johnson, British historian and author, lists five marks of a great leader. Included in that list is humor. He states that he can think of very few truly great leaders who were devoid of humor and cites Presidents Abraham Lincoln and Ronald Reagan as those who virtually governed through their sense of humor. Their homespun, pointed quips were hard to miss and easy to understand.

The nine most terrifying words in the English language are: "I'm from the government and I'm here to help."
—President Ronald Reagan

Surprisingly, a lot has been written in recent years concerning the effectiveness of leading with a good sense of humor. Any woman in any leadership role certainly has a wealth of humor material at her fingertips. Just walk in your own shoes for a day, and you'll be qualified to try out for *Comedy Central*! Good leaders understand that a leader who is balanced in her approach will be able to see the humor in life and work situations. Peter Jonas, the chair of Leadership Studies at Cardinal Stritch University, has written and spoken extensively about the ways humor can be used to a leader's advantage in many venues. He suggests a leader can use humor in the following ways:

- to build teamwork
- to put individuals at ease
- to learn how to read team members and followers
- to break down barriers between leaders and followers
- to present situations and problems in a humorous light and to diffuse "hot" responses
- to help people remember important information

How many leaders does it take to change a light bulb? One: she stands on her chair, holds up the light bulb and waits for the world to revolve around her!

If you are honest enough to say your sense of humor is not very well developed, hold on—there's hope for you. Jonas has several tips to develop your sense of humor.

- Choose jokes that are practical and address common experiences. (If you are speaking to a group of women, don't tell a sports joke!)

- Practice the jokes ahead of time, and try them with friends.
- Be as original as possible with the jokes. (Old *Reader's Digest* issues have great material.)
- Personalize the joke when possible.
- Less is more, i.e., tell the story, give the punch line and get out.
- Be enthusiastic.
- The point of humor is to teach and to create a warm, welcoming atmosphere.

Let me illustrate the personalization of a story/joke. I heard a great joke about a little boy in the grocery store with his mother. He noticed a large woman in the aisle and commented on her weight. His mother hushed him, and they moved to another aisle. When they got into the checkout line, the same woman was in front of them. Her cell phone began to ring. Startled, the little guy said, "Look out, Mom; she's backing up!" Now, I thought this was hilarious but not wanting to insult any woman in the audience, I decided to make the story about my husband who is currently fighting a weight battle. I didn't offend anyone, the story was well received, and my husband didn't mind. (He knows he's fat!)

When a woman uses her sense of humor and continues to develop it for use in her leadership roles, she is taking advantage of a natural way to relate to people. As she conducts meetings, makes presentations, gives reports, enlists volunteers, and presents important information, she can be more confident and at ease with humor "by her side." Because humor can cross barriers, its use can build a feeling of unity. It can make the difference between disaster and working something out in a highly volatile situation. It is a good practice to look for ways to interject humor into tense, anxious settings.

Working women are often tested as leaders when they are teased by their male co-workers. While a woman shouldn't engage in off-color humor (remember working from convictions?), she needs to exhibit her confidence by allowing herself to be teased and even teasing back. Humor in the workplace, if appropriate, can be a morale booster and build teamwork. As in other situations, caution is necessary to ensure that the humor is appropriate to the situation. A joke or quip should be brief and not aggressive (no put-downs). Never disguise criticism with humor as that results in misunderstanding and hurt feelings.

Well, this is a lot of information about laughter and a sense of humor. Is it really that important to a balanced leadership approach? Actually, yes! Studies have revealed that the vast majority of organizations look specifically for leaders with a sense of humor, because it helps to build positive organizational culture. Leaders with a sense of humor tend to be more creative and apt to accept change more readily. They are able to laugh at the mistakes they make and at themselves, which relaxes others. This in no way means that these leaders do not take their work or their goals seriously. The goals for the work at hand can still be achieved but with a lighter, more joyful approach.

As a woman leads a task force at work or a project for PTA (Parent Teacher Association) at her child's school, her sense of humor will help her relate to others, create a "user-friendly" climate, and encourage those around her to respond to life and work from a lighter perspective. There is no such thing as a person who can't be funny— only those who are not willing to try.

Middle age is when your age starts to show around your middle.
—Bob Hope

For Sale: Wedding dress, size 8. Worn once by mistake.

An elderly couple went into a restaurant and because they had no reservation, they were told there would be a 45-minute wait. "Now see here, we're both 90 years old and we may not have 45 minutes!" They were seated immediately.

Equipoise—A leader needs to learn to laugh at herself, with others, and to understand how humor can diffuse difficult leadership situations. To laugh or not is your choice.

God's Symmetry—*He who is of a merry heart has a continual feast.*
—Proverbs 15:15 (NKJV)

Tipping the Scales—Can we as leaders manufacture some laughs? Yes! Try these ideas: find a humor/joke book and read it; watch old episodes of *I Love Lucy* or your favorite comedy movies; look for the absurdity in situations and relate it to someone else; spend time with people who look on the bright side; remind yourself to have fun.

Notes

Prayerfully review the chapter.

What is God calling you to do?

How can the lessons of this chapter help you become a better leader?

What steps do you need to take next?

4

Did You Say What I Thought You Said?

◇◇◇◇◇◇◇◇

Let your conversation be always full of grace,
seasoned with salt, so that you may know
how to answer everyone.
—Colossians 4:6 (TNIV)

◇◇◇◇◇◇◇◇

Before we were married, my husband and I spent hour after hour just talking to each other. We both had a lot to say and wanted to learn all we could about each other. Neither of us had a car nor any money, so our dates consisted of walking. We would walk mile after mile, hand in hand, "talking things over." Coming from very different backgrounds, it was important that we understood each other's point of view about things and the "whys" of those views. Occasionally, our date would end at our favorite local college hangout with a soft drink. Sometimes it ended with a soft drink from the on-campus vending machine. Most of the time, however, we just walked through neighborhoods near the college campus. Years later, we retraced one rambling walk in a car and discovered that we'd walked seven miles! That was a lot of time invested in communicating. True, financial issues played a part in that, but we really were interested in each other's dreams, thoughts, and plans for the future. These walking talks helped to cement our relationship and give us a strong foundation for marriage.

Now married for many years, our level of communication has only strengthened. But, even though we spend hours communicating with each other there is no guarantee that we will always understand what the other is saying or trying to say! There are the normal misunderstandings, frustrations, and communication issues that are common to all married couples. And through the years of marriage, we have learned what those "unspoken" words mean; what the silences are meant to convey; and how to mend fences and rebuild bridges in the area of communication.

I have chosen a sheet of newspaper for the symbol of this chapter, because it is such a universal and everyday form of communication. However, while the impact of printed sources is tremendous on our lives, most of our attention in this chapter will focus on the spoken word as it communicates our beliefs, opinions, and keeps us in touch with our day-to-day world. Learning to communicate is a daunting endeavor that impacts every woman's life. Whether it is "getting through" to her husband or children, making an important presentation at work, or leading a small group, effective communication is critical.

Am I Getting Through?

I'd like to tell a personal story that illustrates just how critical communication is to our daily lives. Several years ago, I began to notice that my husband was ignoring some rather important things that the children and I were saying. He became more and more unresponsive, and it concerned everyone. The kids didn't get what was happening to their dad's personality and why he had become so remote. Never having had any relatives who were hearing impaired, that possibility never crossed our minds. Little did we know what a journey lay ahead of us. During the next ten years, we experienced tremendous upheaval in our home and lives. My husband's hearing began taking "dives" every six months or so until his hearing, with powerful hearing aids, registered at two percent in one ear and four percent in the other. In case you don't know—that's deaf!

The process of losing his hearing was traumatic for everyone, and major adjustments had to be made in every area of our lives. He wasn't the only one with a hearing problem! We all shared in his hearing loss. An excellent conversationalist became a recluse, because he couldn't hear what was going on. An active deacon, he resigned because he couldn't follow the conversation in meetings. Teaching a Bible study class became an ordeal. Listening to music was a thing of the past. Attending any kind of recital or drama or school event was something to be endured. He did (and still does) go to "chick flicks" with me but just to keep me company! While my husband's company was willing to make the concessions required by the American with Disabilities Act, his immediate supervisor was very difficult.

Eventually, my husband had cochlear implant surgery after failing all the correct tests. It was a very successful implant, enabling him to go back to work and our lives began to return to some semblance of normalcy. The implant was a blessing directly from God Himself. Not only was it successful, our medical insurance paid every penny of the expenses.

The full benefits were short-lived, however. On his way to a work appointment, Jan was injured in an automobile accident. The ultimate result was damage to his implant, and he lost 3 of his 19 "channels" and developed permanent vertigo. Being forced to take an early disability retirement was not anything we had ever anticipated or planned for. New adjustments were added to the ones we had been making for ten years. Nonetheless, the implant has enabled Jan to teach in controlled situations, to take in an occasional action movie (he's a superb lip reader!), and to hold his own in most conversations.

I hope this story underlines the importance of communication. Just because someone sees our lips moving and is looking at us and seemingly giving us her attention is not a guarantee that communication is taking place. Living with a hearing-impaired person changes how you communicate—that's for sure! What our three children and I have learned through the years matches with everything that I've read on the subject of communication. While being hearing impaired brings special circumstances to the table, some of the principles are applicable in all communication settings. I've even heard women say that their husbands don't have an official hearing problem but they are certain they have selective hearing!

Here, from my personal point of view, are some tips I've learned about communication:

- Look at the person to whom you are speaking.
- Don't drop your head or your voice while speaking.
- Speak clearly at all times.
- Rephrase anything that might be confusing. Choose your words carefully.
- Ask questions to confirm that the hearer has understood what you've just said.
- Minimize barriers to understanding when possible: eliminate shadows on your face; watch your drawl and accent; face the light.
- Watch hand movements that cross your face.
- Minimize moving around while speaking.
- Beware of mustaches and wide-brimmed hats!

Here's a more light-hearted look at the importance of effective communication. Listen in on what is being said:

"So did you have a nice birthday over the weekend?"

"Well, actually we didn't do much. Our daughter came over Saturday night and we had cake and ice cream."

"Oh, that was nice. Did she bake the cake?"

"Not likely! No, she picked it up at the grocery store on her way over. Dan called her to do it, because he forgot."

Awaken the Leader in You

"Well, at least you had a cake!"

"That's true, but it was chocolate, and I guess no one remembered I'm not supposed to eat chocolate. I just ate the ice cream."

"I like your sweater; was it a birthday gift?"

"No, well actually, I guess you could say it was. I bought it for myself. I figured that would be the only gift I'd get, so I just charged it on our credit card. Thanks for mentioning it, especially since it turned out to be the only thing I got that I really liked."

"Oh, did Dan forget that too? I would have thought he'd remember the date after all the years you've been married."

"Well, he got me the usual gift certificate to the department store, but it won't be enough to get what I'd really like to buy."

"What is it that you want so badly?"

"Well, I've always wished and hoped that Dan would buy me one of those pearl droplet necklaces. It doesn't have to be terribly expensive. It's just that I've never had one."

"Why hasn't he bought one? My impression of Dan is that he can be thoughtful. Does he think it's a waste of money or what?"

"Oh, um, the thing is . . . Dan doesn't know that I want the necklace."

"Let me be sure I understand here . . . . Dan hasn't bought the necklace you really, really want but he doesn't know you want it? How's that possible?"

"I just assumed he would figure out how much I wanted it and get it for me. I've never actually asked for it."

"Do you think that's why he's never given it to you? Is he a mind reader, and I didn't know it? How in the world would you ever think he would buy the necklace if you hadn't told him how much you'd love to have it? I don't understand!"

When true communication takes place, there is an understanding of what has been said, the reasoning behind the statements, and insight into what a process involves or what action needs to take place. From the account above, you can see that while the friend used good communication skills, the woman who wanted the necklace was clueless about what good communication involves.

Let's now examine an entirely different communication scenario from the Bible.

Biblical Snapshot

Priscilla and her husband, Aquila, came into Paul's life when he traveled from Athens to Corinth. The couple had left Rome because of an edict that Claudius had issued for all Jews to leave Rome. Since they, too, were tentmakers, Paul worked with them and stayed with them. When Paul left Corinth to go to Ephesus, Priscilla and Aquila traveled with him. They stayed in Ephesus even after Paul moved on. We believe that they had begun working with Paul among the group of believers in the city. Acts 18 introduces a new arrival on the religious scene—Apollos. Apollos was a Jew and a native of Alexandria. Scripture says he was a powerful and eloquent speaker and preacher. He evidently had a good grasp of the Scripture. However, Acts 18:25 records that *"Apollos was accurate in everything he taught about Jesus up to a point, but he only went as far as the baptism of John."* Priscilla and Aquila heard Apollos speak in the synagogue and knew he needed to hear what they had learned from Paul.

The couple invited Apollos to their home to explain to him the ways of God more fully. Luke names Priscilla as the primary instructor on this occasion. From this we

---

can gather that she was an intelligent, articulate woman who had studied enough under Paul to gain knowledge that would benefit Apollos. Scripture credits her with being the teacher of the eloquent Apollos. Even though the account in Acts is a brief one, I believe three communication skills can be attributed to Priscilla.

First, when Priscilla heard Apollos speaking and realized that what he was preaching was incomplete, she didn't interrupt him and object to what he was *not* saying. She listened before responding. Second, Priscilla was skilled in making others understand what she was saying. The verses in Acts indicate that she not only taught Apollos, she expounded, which is an indication that she was knowledgeable and was skilled at imparting information so that others understood. She chose her words carefully, words that had specific meaning, and she was clear in presenting the news about Jesus that Apollos obviously didn't have.

Third, Priscilla demonstrated her skill as a communicator when she realized it would be inappropriate to correct Apollos in public. Many times people in places of leadership feel compelled to correct and criticize everyone on the spot. She opened her home and extended hospitality to Apollos. Her instruction was done in private without being condescending.

Priscilla had the opportunity to show everyone how much she knew and how capable she was. She could have spoken with authority and insight and taken the stage, so to speak, away from Apollos. That is not what she chose to do, however. She shared her knowledge with Apollos in a nonthreatening way and with a helpful spirit. Priscilla is a good example of an effective communicator, because she was sensitive to what the outcome could be if she approached Apollos in love. His influence as he preached would increase through her instruction. Perhaps Priscilla was familiar with Proverbs 18:13 *"To answer before listening—that is folly and shame"* (TNIV). Maybe she had heard Paul quote Proverbs 12:18, *"Rash language cuts and maims, but there is healing in the words of the wise."*

Priscilla can serve as a communications role model today. She had reached the conclusion that what she said and how she said it were important and that she could serve God effectively through her communication.

Communication Style

I knew my ideas were good. I had carefully crafted them to support the purpose and outcome of the major project we had been assigned. I typed up my notes and arranged my presentation so that it was logical and flowed well. I was armed with samples, statistics, and my creativity demonstrated my commitment to the project's importance. I arrived at our meeting early and distributed copies of my ideas so everyone could follow my comments easily. Everyone arrived and the meeting began. When the time for my report came, I enthusiastically made my presentation, outlining the logic behind my suggestions. I was friendly, maintained eye contact, finished within my time allotment, and asked for questions. The person who had the primary responsibility for the project remained silent. His facial expression revealed nothing. Outwardly, he exhibited no response to a single thing I had said. It was almost as if he wasn't there even though I could see him sitting in his chair!

When the silence became awkward, I ventured to ask, "Those are my ideas, Rob (not his real name). What are your thoughts?" With a shake of his head, he seemed to struggle to focus his eyes and replied, "I'm not sure. I'll have to think everything over." I felt as if the time I had invested in research and creative thinking had been a waste. It seems almost ridiculous to state the obvious here—this co-worker was known as a person who did not communicate effectively. When he did respond, it was often negatively. He had a poor grip on his emotions and was easily sidetracked, which resulted in missing important parts of what someone was saying.

Could you write a similar scenario from your experience at work or from your involvement as a volunteer in a community organization? Perhaps you have encountered someone like Rob on a committee in your church. Maybe something like this has happened with your teenager at home, resulting in a misunderstanding. As women, it may sometimes seem as if we (at least at home) are looked upon as the "clearinghouse" for all family communications. Do we look like a bulletin board where everyone posts their messages? Are we are to relay each and every message to other members of the family? Achieving balance in this critical part of life can be somewhat of an overwhelming task. Playing games like "He said, she said" and "But I thought you realized that" can be tiresome, dangerous, and unproductive.

Most women want to become better communicators. One way to become more effective in this area is to take a CI (communication inventory). Ask yourself the following questions to determine what your communication style is and how others see it. Your answers may help you assess what you need to learn or repair as you communicate at home, with neighbors, at church, where you work, or in community settings.

1. List three words that describe how you communicate at home. Make another list to describe how you communicate in another situation. Are the lists the same?

2. How would people close to you describe how you communicate?

3. This is harder—ask six persons with whom you work (church, community, volunteer capacity, etc.) this question: What three adjectives would you use to describe how I communicate?

4. What are the similarities between the words used by people close to you and those used by persons with whom you work?

5. Choose one situation and decide on an action you are going to take to improve your communication.

6. Determine how you will monitor improvement (ask someone to observe you).

Does this sound like a lot of work? It will be, but remember the result will make you a more effective communicator!

Because communication is so essential to a balanced life, libraries and bookstores have shelves crammed with resources about the subject. The Internet is a wealth of information, and even popular magazines have joined the parade in telling us the importance of clear communication, how to maximize our communication efforts, and the benefits of connecting to others. Communication is too important a part of daily life to be disregarded. You cannot *not* communicate. In the case of my co-worker, his failure to speak words did not mean he wasn't communicating. He said volumes by his body language (he was bored), by his lack of facial expression (he didn't care), and by his unresponsiveness (he really hadn't listened).

The way others interpret what we say at work may affect our career advancement. The manner in which something is said in a church business session may cause disharmony in Christ's body. Misunderstandings between what a wife thinks she said and what her husband says she said can wreck a marriage. The television commercial in which the wife asks her husband, "Does this dress make me look fat?" only to receive his inattentive "Uh huh" response illustrates how poor communication can hurt a relationship.

If communication is so vital, so critical, what does the Bible say about our conversation and how we are to relate to others through verbal and nonverbal speech? Various categories emerge when you begin to look at the many verses of instruction we are to follow if we want to be godly communicators and maintain healthy relationships with those around us. Take time to look up and read the passages that are listed here. God's Word is not silent on how we are to treat others with our speech.

Words are powerful: Proverbs 18:21; 15:1; 10:32; Ephesians 4:29.

Words can get you into trouble: Proverbs 6:2; 12:23; 13:17; 18:8; 21:23.

Our speech should be uplifting: Proverbs 16:24; 15:23; 12:14; 10:11, 20; Titus 2:8.

Non-verbal communication "speaks" volumes: eyes—2 Kings 8:11; face—Genesis 4:6; hands—1 Timothy 2:8; kiss—1 Corinthians 16:20; touch—Mark 10:13.

Jesus' skill as a communicator gives us the best possible role model. Look at your communication style and see how (or if) it parallels His style.

- Jesus engaged others in conversation.
- Jesus asked a lot of questions.
- Jesus was approachable and accessible.
- Jesus made a connection with others.
- Jesus listened to what people had to say.

A Fine Art

Our oldest granddaughter and her father were in the car going somewhere alone. Our son was giving Catelyn instructions as they drove along. This went on for several minutes until finally in frustration Catelyn said loudly from the backseat, "Dad! You're telling me stuff, and Mom's telling me stuff. My head's so full my brain won't work!"

Sound familiar? When we begin thinking about all the parts of communication and how important clear communication is, and when we consider that words can hurt, maim, and demoralize, we may be tempted to say, "What's the use? There's no way I can master the fine art of communication." There is the truth in a nutshell so to speak—communication is just that, a fine art. As women, we communicate every day, all day long. We communicate ideas, emotions, opinions, beliefs, and even love. We do this with words but also with our facial expressions and posture. There are many factors involved in communicating clearly, and most of them have been discussed in depth in other sources. However, since none of us is a perfect communicator, it might be of value to review some of the basics of communication.

Being a good communicator means . . .
- that you think before you speak.
- that you resist distractions when listening to someone else speak.
- that you maintain eye contact when speaking and listening.
- that you concentrate on what's being said.
- that you avoid forming how you will respond before the speaker is finished.

Most women realize the impact everyday communication mishaps and successes have on their lives; likewise they recognize the need for this "fine art" in the leadership world also. James Humes said, "The art of communication is the language of leadership." If his statement is true, then Lorin Woolfe in *Leadership Secrets from the Bible* is not too bold when he says, "A leader who cannot communicate clearly, powerfully and succinctly barely qualifies as a leader." While at first glance this seems harsh, it is food for thought as we consider the responsibilities a woman has as she seeks to lead and lead effectively.

I thought it would be interesting to approach some specific issues regarding communication in leadership through the use of equations.

Message Sent ≠ Message Received

We explain something, make a request, or give instructions, and then ask, "Do you understand?" When we receive a positive response, we move on, making the assumption that our message was received. Such is not always the case, however! The truth of the matter is that while we believe we have been perfectly clear, the "receiver" has interpreted our comments in a very different way than we intended.

This could be true for several reasons. Perhaps the person has a short attention span so what we said didn't "click." If we use ambiguous language or terminology, it can cloud the meaning. What if I had just said "woolly terminology?" Would you have thought I was talking about sheep? The use of unfamiliar jargon can also result in misinterpretation. When a doctor uses medical jargon, his explanation often goes right over our heads. The terms mechanics use when they try to explain to us what's wrong with our cars leave us clueless. We don't expect to understand them! But in normal conversation, jargon is used with the assumption everyone knows what we mean.

For example, the other day we were in an electronic store to look at replacing my husband's outdated laptop computer. The young man began a rapid-fire description of all the capabilities of the new machine as if we understood every word he said. The fact of the matter is we caught about one out of three! His use of computer jargon was like a foreign language to us. He sent the message; we definitely did not receive it.

Different languages and cultures can further complicate the communication process. People with very different backgrounds may have trouble connecting. Body language too can be very distracting and can hamper the reception of our message. Years ago, while serving as preschool division director for a large church, I worked to enlist parents to serve once a month as volunteers on Sundays and Wednesdays. Our church had a large deaf congregation, and I dealt with parents who were deaf but whose children were hearing. When I first began working with the deaf parents, they had a great deal of trouble figuring out what I was saying even though most of them read lips. The problem arose because I talk so much with my hands. They were trying to read my sign language only I wasn't saying anything with my hands! My body language was confusing the issue.

As we lead, we must strive to ensure that our messages are properly received and understood by everyone with whom we work.

− = + (Less Is More)

How could less ever be more? Think back to all the long, boring presentations you have heard and all the pointless seminars you have attended. Computer presentations with endless charts and statistics begin to blur after the first ten slides. When a speaker, after 20 minutes of rambling, says, "Now here's what I really wanted to tell you," she has already lost her audience. Sometimes, as women we tend to believe that if a little bit is good, more has to be better. Not always so.

As you prepare for a task force report at work or plan to make a presentation before the city council, remember several things: don't give too many dates, facts, or statistics; abide by your time allotment; consider your audience and speak to them; practice your presentation; dress appropriately; and establish rapport with the audience immediately with your opening statement. Be intentional about communicating through everything you do.

Data Dump + Mushy Messages = No Connection

When leading a seminar or delivering a speech, don't overwhelm your audience with information (verbally or with handouts). Don't distribute photocopies unless you will have time to reference them. If you are leading a small group, do not give them all the answers. As leader, it is your responsibility to help your audience learn to think and to ask questions. Their need and interest in participating is one reason they have joined the group, so you need to meet that need. You may believe you are communicating effectively, but you may just be "spoon-feeding." This kind of communication is very limiting and results in little connection with others. Think back to the teacher you liked the best—was it someone who made you think and encouraged your input or one who just fed you information and expected you to "spew" it back?

FROM: CEO's office

MEMO: We wanted you to know that in light of the current situation a strategy has been developed and will be implemented with due diligence in the near future. The results that are expected will not be known for some time but that has no bearing on our ability to foresee that such actions need to occur. We are counting on all of you to facilitate the process so that the company will be able to maintain the focus we believe we should have.

Did you get all of that? What in the world did it mean? Was there a connection between the CEO and his employees?

What strategy? Due diligence? The current situation? What process? As leaders, we get so caught up in our rhetoric and grandiose plans that we send mushy messages that have absolutely no meaning for those we are trying to lead. If women want to communicate clearly, their messages must be clearly stated and the meanings clarified. If we fail to do this, there will be no connection.

High-Tech Equipment – Expertise + Murphy's Law = Disaster

The "siren" of high-tech capabilities draws many leaders to create what they hope will be stellar presentations using their laptops and color copiers. While all the bells and whistles and computer-generated graphics may add flair to a leader's speech, seminar, or meeting, we need to remember that the message is *not* in the technology. It is in you, the leader!

The "minus" in this equation enters when we try to use programs or options beyond our skill, experience, or expertise most of us try to use the technology to our advantage. The success of any high-tech presentation will be in direct proportion to the user's ability to operate equipment and to anticipate problems. Practice your presentation ahead of time so that you are completely at ease with the mechanics. Be sure you have extra bulbs, extension cords, and a backup plan. Using your own equipment will lessen the chance of failure.

I'd say in about one-half of the presentations I have seen over the years, Murphy's Law surfaces. "If anything can go wrong, it will." The real problem is that many times the leader is unprepared to move on without her presentation aids. Too much time is wasted trying to reboot, repair, reconnect, or reset. The audience's attention is gone and the teachable moment has passed. Disaster is the frequent result. Remember the information needs to be in your head and heart, not just in the computer.

An Agenda + Detailed Information − Rambling = Productive Meetings

As a leader it will often be your responsibility to conduct meetings. Not too many people actually like meetings, did you know that? So, first, consider other options. Would sending everyone an email accomplish the same thing as a meeting? If so, don't meet. Will a memo or phone call suffice? If so, don't meet. Don't meet if the real purpose behind meeting is to send a message to one or two people. Use another way to address the issue.

So, you are leading a meeting. An agenda will help your group, committee, or team stay focused. Take care not to have too many items on the agenda as that tends to discourage everyone before you begin. Give enough details in your meeting to facilitate intelligent decision-making. Too many details may cause confusion and might actually create debate over unimportant issues. If you as the leader do not have detailed information, then perhaps you need to meet at another time.

Too many meetings start but don't go anywhere! They take on a life of their own, and it seems they will never end. You, as leader, must assign a time limit to each agenda item. It makes no sense to spend 20 minutes discussing when the next meeting will be! State that to facilitate the meeting, each item will be discussed but will be limited to a specific time. Encourage participation but maintain control over the direction the discussion takes. A skilled communicator can make everyone feel their input is important while still keeping the group focused.

An agenda coupled with complete information and limited "rabbit chasing" can result in a productive meeting. A productive meeting pays good dividends as your team of co-workers, your neighborhood watch group, or your women's Bible study group makes plans to increase influence and impact others.

Formulas, equations, and solutions—all of this sounds rather cold and mathematical, doesn't it? However, these tips and techniques are just means to an end. Good communication is about relationship. And relationship is the heart of leadership. Without well-developed communication skills we cannot hope to be effective leaders.

> *The greatest gift you can give another is the purity of your attention.*
> —Richard Moss, visionary, teacher, and author

Equipoise—As a woman learns to communicate more effectively, she will achieve more balance in her life.

God's Symmetry—*My beloved brethren, let every man be swift to hear, slow to speak, slow to wrath.*
—James 1:19 (NKJV)

Tipping the Scales—*Others tell; leaders sell. Others impress; leaders influence. Others try to be heard; leaders strive to be understood. Others explain; leaders energize. Others inform; leaders inspire. Others relay only facts; leaders tell stories.*
—Mark Sanborn, best-selling author and speaker

Just for Fun

See if you can match these communication words from bygone days with their meanings.

vaniloquence	1. debate
word-pecker	2. suited to public speaking
lip-labour	3. talking foolishly
orotund	4. speak like a bird
stultiloquent	5. empty talk, vain repetition
tongue-fence	6. vain talk
twee	7. one who plays with words

(source: Oxford English Dictionary Online)

Notes

Prayerfully review the chapter.

What is God calling you to do?

How can the lessons of this chapter help you become a better leader?

What steps do you need to take next?

5

Definition of Pressure: "A Mummy Pressed for Time"

◇◇◇◇◇◇◇◇

When I am overwhelmed,
you alone know the way I should turn.
—Psalm 142:3 (NLT)

◇◇◇◇◇◇◇◇

In my dream, I was standing in the middle of a circle of people, all of whom I knew. My husband was there and so were my three children. My parents were both there, and I recognized my pastor and my supervisor from work. My grandchildren were even there! On the ground in the circle was a life-sized, color photograph of me. Outside the circle, I could just barely see a shadowy figure that stepped forward and handed a very large pair of shears to my husband. My husband took the shears, picked up the photograph, and cut off a big piece. He handed the shears to the kids who in turn each cut off a piece of the photo. The shears were passed around the circle until everyone (even the grandchildren!) had taken a piece of my photo. Eventually, there was nothing remaining but the pieces in everyone's hands. Right before my eyes I had become a fragmented woman! (Author's adaptation of a story told by Peg Rankin in *How to Care For the Whole World and Still Take Care of Yourself*.)

This fictitious account could just as easily have happened to me or any number of my friends. In fact, I meet fragmented women all the time! A lot of them are like me in the respect that they have bitten off more than they can chew and don't know what to do with what is on their plates. In this chapter we will focus on the pressure and stresses that come into our lives, some of which we can control and some we can't. However, I need to say early on that not all pressure is bad. We do need to learn to control the stresses within our power to control. But some of the pressure that comes our way as part of normal, everyday life is helpful and cannot be eliminated. The more important thing is that we *can* decide how we will respond to all pressures.

If either of my grandmothers had lived to see the era of home computers, they would have had a difficult time believing that we now have canned air. Used to help us keep our keyboards free of dust, this air, canned under pressure, is a good symbol for this chapter. All too often at the end of a day or in the middle of the week, we resemble a can of air just waiting for someone to come along, press the nozzle, and let us explode right out of the can.

Every individual needs pressure to accomplish the normal activities of life. When the "bad" pressure outweighs the "good" pressure, however, a woman's life balance is skewed. In order to maintain a semblance of balance in her life, a woman needs to be informed about what causes stress (pressure), how to handle that stress, and the dangers of too much stress. The next time you stand for a few minutes in the grocery store checkout line or walk down the "bath" aisle, look at the current products on the market. You'll find a wide assortment of stress relief lotion, stress relief bath/shower gel, bath oils labeled "Relax" and "Stress Relief," and body spray that will calm you and enable you to have a good night's sleep. Do I sound knowledgeable about these products? I have most of them right near my bathtub at home! There are pills to take, lozenges to suck on, drops to put on your tongue, and even gum to chew to help you lessen your stress level.

Aside from making millions of dollars for the manufacturers, why would these products be so popular? Because we are looking for something, anything, to relieve the anxiety, pressure, uncertainty, and burnout feelings we have because of encroaching life situations that leave us drained and emotionally fragile. Could this be the reason for strained marriage relationships, unhappy confrontations with teenagers, displays of temper at work, or disharmony in Christ's church? Some of it can be laid right at the feet of stress, and most of it can be avoided.

Defining the Problem

Before going any further, we should define this word that we are using over and over. One dictionary defines *stress* as "a condition in which an individual fails to makes a satisfactory adaptation." The word *stress* is synonymous with strain, pressure, and tension. The Latin root of the word is "strengere," meaning to bind tight. Stress is any bit of sensory information that gets into the brain and changes the brain's communication to the body. This could be something that angers, hurries, troubles, aggravates, challenges, excites, threatens, upsets, or criticizes. When (not *if*) tension builds, there must be a release. That's where the trouble comes in. Be assured if the tension builds, it will release!

You know, and I know, that each of us releases stress in different ways. My brother and I are very different when it comes to stress relief. I'm more the exploding teapot type while he "brews." When I let off steam, I'm done; I move on. When my brother is under pressure, he thinks it over for a while, lets it steam a bit, before releasing his tension. I was his self-appointed boss when we were children. After all, I *was* the oldest so I should be boss. I could push him just so far, and then his eyes would literally flash and turn red. That's when I'd run! We all have different levels of manageable pressure and release the tension differently.

With this in mind, let's look at some statistics and facts about stress.

Facts about Stress

Here are some statistics courtesy of the American Psychological Association's Web site:

- *Fifty-four percent* of Americans are concerned about the level of stress in their everyday lives.
- A majority of workers (*52 percent*) are more stressed because of work than home.
- *Fifty-four percent* of workers are concerned about health problems caused by stress.
- More than *19 million* American adults have an anxiety disorder.
- Women are more likely than men to have an anxiety disorder.
- Anxiety disorders frequently co-occur with depressive disorders, eating disorders, or substance abuse.

(sources: first three, 2004 APA survey; second three, National Institutes of Mental Health)

Now let's look at the effects of stress on our lives. Physical symptoms of being overstressed include headache, sleep disorders, upset stomach, low morale, anxiety, fatigue, racing heart, jaw pain, blurred vision, shakiness. There's more—grinding teeth, sweaty palms, shoulder and back pain, shortness of breath, nausea, crying easily, eating too much or too little. Then there's the emotional toll: anger, sadness, depression, feeling overwhelmed, inability to concentrate, nervous laugh. And here are some interpersonal effects of stress: complaining, sensitivity to noise, raising voice in conversation, late arrival to appointments, missed meetings, conflict with others, can't think or write.

These lists remind me of the woman who had had a terrible week at work, and home life hadn't been pretty either. She came home one night and the family dog barked to get her attention. Thinking he wanted outside, she went to the door but she realized in amazement, "The dog asked *me* to leave!" Have you been there? Last week you say? If we recognize that our behavior and our response to the pressures of life affect us so adversely physically, emotionally, and in our relating to others, what can women do to control their response to stress?

Before we can begin formulating remedies and determining solutions, we need to discover what it is in a woman's life that creates stress. There are several stress tests you can take that will show you what causes most of the tension in your life. It might be in your best interest—you know, to relieve some pressure—if you go to your public library and find a book that contains one of these surveys. The last time I took a stress test my score was so high I realized why a women's council had asked me to lead a seminar on stress! Since that time, I have become more adept at dealing with the pressures I face, and I am more careful about allowing new stressors to come into my life. I'm not always successful, but at least I'm doing a better job than before.

Which of the following stress points are in your life?

- Lack of sufficient time to get things done
- Children of any age
- A husband
- Financial issues
- Housework
- Career (inside or outside of the home)

These six areas (above) have been identified as major stress points in most women's lives. The stress connected to any of these will be magnified if any of the following issues are also present.

Anger—Women pay a high price for controlling their anger at all costs. We are taught that anger is unladylike, and it is our job to placate and protect our world. Can you see how anger related to children could create tension? Toward a co-worker who received the promotion you wanted?

Painful emotions—Guilt, fear, and jealousy can make us do foolish things. Do you see how these emotions can cause tension in a marital relationship? Could guilt motivate us to make unwise financial decisions?

Grief—Grief must be dealt with in a healthy way. We must recognize that anger is part of grief and accept it. Letting the tears flow and expressing anger in constructive ways will help alleviate the pressure. Grief is not limited to loss from death. It might be the result of any major loss such as losing a job, making a physical move, or going through a divorce.

Job stress—Most of job-related stress is beyond our control. The majority of women who work do so out of financial need. It doesn't matter if a woman has a full-time career, works part time, or has her own business at home, she will still have job-related tensions.

If just reading about the causes of stress has increased your stress, it may be time for you to move away from situations that are keeping you off balance in your life. Identifying the areas where most of the pressure is coming from is a step in the right direction. If we will do what the writer says in Psalm 46:10, we will be ready to make some choices to minimize our stress level. *"Step out of the traffic! Take a long, loving look at me, your High God, above politics, above everything.*" Step out of the traffic and read on for some possible solutions to your stress dilemma.

Do Not Play by These Rules

First, let's look at some typical ways we can get sucked into the game of stress (and some steps to get out).

Game of Stress Rule #1

Deny that we create our own stress. We want to believe that stress could never happen to us. We spend too much time trying to fix situations and not enough in preventing them. We do this because we don't like to wait for anything. Scientific reports indicate that when adrenaline is produced, the body can't tell the difference between good stress and bad stress. We get "hooked" on the excitement and the adrenaline rush. To keep your stress level up, continue denying you have it.

Game of Stress Rule #2

Cancel our vacations, due to pressure at work, and cut back on our celebrating. There is always something that can interfere with our taking a much-needed break. We need to be honest with ourselves and others about how much downtime we need. Celebrating brings joy and perspective about what is really important in life. When we don't celebrate and take time off, we are still playing the game of stress.

Game of Stress Rule #3

Believe there is nothing we can do to lessen some of the tension at work. Small things can make a difference in a workday: take a walk during your lunch break rather than staying inside in the same surroundings; do some simple exercises during the day at your desk; spritz lavender water on your face (it has a calming ingredient); delegate more; and prioritize your assignments. Proverbs 10:17 says it best, *"The road to life is a disciplined life."* Stress at work may come because we are disorganized, spend our time unwisely, or are distracted. Can we make our own stress? Sometimes.

Game of Stress Rule #4
Become a people-pleasing, attention-seeking martyr. When we want to please everyone, we are setting ourselves up for failure and unwarranted pressure. When we catch ourselves trying to smooth everything over and exhibiting an "it's my fault" attitude, we need to stop apologizing for everything and learn to say no. This is not to say we shouldn't accept responsibility for things that are our fault, but we can deflect tension by not assuming guilt for things we didn't do! When we crave attention and thrive on praise, we need to see this for the immature behavior that it is. Don't accept the tension this brings; put someone else in the spotlight. Remember the television commercial about the mother giving away the last crispy marshmallow treat? With a huge martyr's sigh she says, "Go ahead...take the last one. I'll make more." Women often get trapped into believing they must be martyrs by letting everyone walk all over them and abuse them. (This is not a reference to physical or verbal abuse.) To exit the game of stress, take positive steps to build self-esteem, stop being a martyr, and try not to assume responsibility for everyone else.

Game of Stress #5
Ignore upcoming deadlines and turn a blind eye to stress triggers. Deadlines, family conflict, financial matters, and health issues create tension. Deadlines are not always creators of bad stress. What would happen if April 15 was just a suggestion to taxpayers? Deadlines represent the good stress that motivates us to perform in a responsible and timely way. So we can't procrastinate and pretend we didn't see the deadline coming. Setting deadlines within a deadline breaks the task down into manageable pieces and lessens stress. We all know that financial difficulties raise the pressure level as you grapple with insurance payments, car repair bills, and orthodontist fees. But we can also plan in advance for those times. And who of us doesn't feel more stressed when we are ill? If we stop exercising, we are candidates for more tension (Oh, you don't exercise? More on that later!). If we are not maintaining spiritual growth, the stress levels in our lives will increase. Lack of spiritual food will cause imbalance in a Christian woman's life, just as poor nutrition is unhealthy for us physically. Know what sets you up for an increase in tension, and be prepared to manage it.

Game of Stress #6
Worry. Be anxious over everything and stay in the game of stress. Or get out of this game by putting your faith in the One in control. Write out the following verse, put it in your purse, next to your bed, on your bathroom mirror, over the kitchen sink, on your desk, and in your heart, *"First pay attention to me, and then relax. Now you can take it easy—you're in good hands"* (Proverbs 1:33).

Take Action!

Finding information about stress and the way it harms us in many ways is relatively easy. Learning the way to respond to tension more appropriately is really not too hard either. If a woman wants to have balance in her life, there are some practical steps she can take to relieve stress and achieve that balance.

> *God is a God of order, calm, and peace. If I am leading a frenetic life, I'm likely not going to make anybody want what I have in terms of a relationship with Christ.*
> —Lois Flowers, *Women, Faith, and Work*

Most women are list-makers—grocery lists, to-do lists, errand lists, gift-buying lists, honey-do lists, supply lists, and the like. Because women seem to function well from a list, perhaps the following lists will be of help as you try to overcome the factors that cause tension.

How to Handle Stress List
1. Relax—try breathing exercises.
2. Make time for yourself—and don't feel guilty!
3. Get proper sleep.
4. Eat right—fuel up with fruits, proteins, and veggies. Caffeine and sugar are stress triggers along with salt, fat, and high-calorie intake.
5. Exercise—walk, move around, join a health club, and go on a regular basis.
6. Learn to prioritize—major on the majors
7. Help others—focusing on others is healthy.
8. Set limits—establish boundaries.
9. Find something you enjoy doing as a distraction from everyday tension.

10. Plan your time—the best thing you can do is to give God your time. Read Psalm 46, paying close attention to the verses 1–3.
11. Pay attention to your emotional and spiritual needs.
12. Focus less on doing everything and more on what you can do well.
13. Acknowledge what you are obsessive about and move away from it.

Exodus 4 records the story of Moses encountering God in the desert. God asked Moses what was in his hand. He replied that it was a shepherd's rod. God told him to throw the staff on the ground. When he did, the staff turned into a snake. This rod can serve as a visual image of all the things we pick up, inherit, take from other people, and have tossed into our hands. Take a piece of paper and trace around your hand. Inside the drawing, write down all the things in your hands right at this time. You may write names of family or children, time, an ability, and the like. Now, mark off the "snakes" (the things you can let go). Finish reading the story in Exodus, and you'll see that when Moses took the snake by its tail as God instructed, it became a staff again. Isn't that what God does when we yield our concerns to Him? He shows us His power and then helps us move forward in His love.

At the very center of the damage stress causes in women's lives are the implications for spiritual well-being. When a woman has a close relationship with God and has stress under control (at least what she can control), she is calmer, laughs more, and enjoys life to a fuller degree, since it seems life has more meaning. Stress doesn't make any woman attractive! Look at the frazzled, stressed woman. She has a certain look about her as if she'd like to look "put together," but she just can't make it. Her conversation is peppered with negativity, and even her tone of voice says, "I've had all I can take!" She walks as if the weight of the entire world is on her shoulders. Her body needs help but she "doesn't have time to exercise." Her shoulders are rounded from carrying everyone's burdens. Does this describe anyone you know? Did you see her in the mirror this morning?

If women can learn to manage stress in their lives, they will experience more victories than defeats. By making behavioral changes they can leave the stress swamp and have healthier relationships and lead a fuller life as God intended. Many women find themselves in a very hard place—they have little time for anything but work, fewer friendships, less time for family, and no time for themselves. This is a recipe for an out-of-balance life. Someone has said we (women) have learned too well the lesson of how to "flame the taper at both extremities."

It should be no surprise that if a woman's life is out of balance because of stress in her personal life that she will take stress into her leadership life as well. You don't have to be a CEO or chairperson of a large board of directors to experience stress as a leader. There is no leadership position that is free of stress. Leading a team, working with a committee, serving on a ministry or missions group, or marshaling your family out the door for an outing all have the potential for stress.

The Book of Proverbs has much to say about living in "robust sanity." We can only benefit from God's grace and mercy when we live by His standards. Walk with the wise—Proverbs 13:14. Embrace God's ways—Proverbs 8:32–36. Avoid falling to pieces—Proverbs 24:10.

In our attempt to have everything, be everything, and do everything, we are guilty of buying into what some have called the "Esau Syndrome." Women are no exception when it comes to thinking that it's all right to satisfy their short-term appetites and trade away God's promises. Hebrews 12:17 retells the story of how Esau traded his birthright for his father's blessing. When he repented and tried to fix what he had done, he could not take back the choice he had made, although he sought for it with bitter tears. Do you know women leaders who have done some trading they will regret later? Perhaps.

How a woman deals with the stress she encounters in her leadership roles will be a measure of her effectiveness as a leader. Regardless of the kind of position a woman holds, her ability to quickly access a situation and deal with it will speak to her previous preparation. Remember the discussion on being prepared because of a conviction that God wants prepared leaders? (Return to chapter 2 if you skipped that part.)

Just as women become overwhelmed with responsibilities in their personal lives, the same can become true in assuming leadership positions. Becoming involved in PTA as a member can turn into being the coordinator of the annual Christmas Shop (personal experience here!). Joining a missions project group can morph into leading a churchwide trip to the inner city to serve Thanksgiving dinner to the homeless. Leading out in your homeschool district is worthwhile, but do you have the time to spend as the field-trip supervisor? Overcommitment is an easy trap to fall into. Each activity must be scrutinized as to its benefit, value, and priority in your life.

Here's another list for you list-makers:

Dealing with Pressure as a Leader
1. Slow down—take time to read the Bible and pray.
2. Take a close look at how you spend your time.
3. Evaluate what you do—can anything be eliminated?
4. What can you delegate to others?
5. Set priorities.
6. Say yes to priorities and no to other activities.
7. Set aside time to enjoy simple pleasures (walks along the beach, a hike in the woods, a visit to the library).
8. Make thorough plans and develop sound strategies for your leadership role.
9. Develop your sense of humor—leadership demands it!

Incorporating the things listed above into your leadership days will give you balance and help reduce the pressure that arises from the duties and expectations connected to leading. During times of high pressure, a fellow leader and I email back and forth frequently, making plans and decisions regarding leadership training. My friend ends many of her emails with "Where's the chocolate?" or "I need chocolate!" or "Oh no! I'm out of chocolate!" Sometimes the only way to deal with pressures related to leadership is to laugh (that's better than crying, don't you think?)

Guess who said this: "Every now and then go away, have a little relaxation, for when you come back to your work your judgment will be surer. Go some distance away because then the work appears smaller and more of it can be taken in at a glance and a lack of harmony and proportion is more readily seen." (See the end of this chapter for the answer.)

A woman in leadership who has out-of-control pressures is ineffective and in need of balance. That balance can be restored, or at least weighted more positively, by establishing priorities. Let's take a look at a biblical example.

━ Biblical Snapshot ━

The story of Abigail illustrates for us the need to place unquestioning faith in God. 1 Samuel 25 describes Abigail as a *"woman of good understanding"* (AMP) and beauty. In contrast, we are told her husband, Nabal, was *"rough and evil in his doings"* (AMP). Their arranged marriage must have brought a great deal of sorrow to Abigail, as their "mismatch" was obvious. Nabal was out in the field shearing sheep when David sent ten of his young men to ask for food. David told his messengers to tell Nabal that they had done no harm to any of his sheep or shepherds. Nabal's reply was consistent with the kind of man he was. He refused to give David's men anything to drink or eat and sent them back to David with insults ringing in their ears. He made quite a point out of belittling David and his family.

Verse 11 indicates his disdain for their request and emphasizes the self-importance he felt because of all that was his (and would remain his). When David's men reported to him what Nabal had told them, he was furious, and he issued the order to prepare to go and kill Nabal and his entire household. One of Nabal's men reported to Abigail all that had happened. He also told her that David was preparing to seek revenge and destroy all of them. Abigail immediately began making preparations to take food to David and his men.

Abigail could actually have done several things other than what she did. She could have lamented about the sad state of affairs in her marriage to this "brute." She could have wrung her hands in despair and waited for David to appear. Indecisiveness, however, was not an option she considered. She wasted no time, threatened no one. She simply went to work organizing her household to make amends.

Going to David herself, she took the blame for not sending out food to him and his men and asked forgiveness for not seeing the men he had sent asking for food. She didn't dwell on passing the blame to Nabal although she did mention the *"foolish and wicked fellow Nabal"* (AMP). Not crumbling under pressure, Abigail was smart enough to caution David against dong anything that would harm his reputation in the future. She let him know that she saw great things in his future and said, *"Blessed be the lord God of Israel, which sent thee this day to meet me; and blessed be thy advice"* (1 Samuel 25:32–33 KJV).

Looking at Abigail, several things are apparent about her leadership. Even though the very physical lives of her household were in danger, she took immediate action. Her ability to make a quick decision probably saved her life and others' lives. While what she did was noteworthy in everyone's eyes, she was humble and approached David in humility. That, too, is the mark of a leader who can deal with pressure. In addition, her organization also helped deal with the tension. Abigail's skill at gathering 200 loaves of bread, 5 sheep dressed ready to eat, 100 clusters of raisins, 200 fig cakes, and a bushel of roasted grain on short notice was no easy feat!

Abigail serves as an example of a woman in a leadership position (over her family and household) who rose above the circumstances of her life and the pressures thrust on her to change the course of events. She demonstrated intelligence, honesty, courage, faith, and generosity. Someone has said that of all the famous women in the Old Testament she was the wisest. Hundreds of years later, she serves as a role model of successful leadership under pressure.

We have looked at some common causes of stress, its definition, and at the havoc it can produce in our lives. Discovering how to recognize stress makers and how to deal with pressure will enable us to maintain some kind of balance in our personal lives. The lessons we've learned can be applied to our leadership lives as we attempt to be faithful to God's call. Women who hear that call to be leaders in their families, in ministry, among their friends, or in the workplace can lead more effectively if they lead with a conviction that God will take care of the stress.

Equipoise—*The axis of the world doesn't turn on whether you get through that list, accomplish that task, pick up the phone, or answer that question.*
—Leonard Sweet, *SoulSalsa*

Keeping things in perspective will help women stay balanced under pressure.

God's Symmetry—*Do not fret or have any anxiety about anything, but in every circumstance and in everything by prayer and petition with thanksgiving continue to make your wants known to God.*
—Philippians 4:6 (AMP)

Tipping the Scales—Be there; concentrate on the present. Let it go. Dissect, change, modify; then let it go. Do your best. Expand your horizons. When all else fails, my personal favorite is to take a sheet of plastic bubble wrap and have a popping session! My son-in-law thanks me profusely for passing this tip on to my daughter.

*Answer to Quote: The "timely" quote on page 108 is from Leonardo da Vinci, 1452–1519.

Notes

Prayerfully review the chapter.

What is God calling you to do?

How can the lessons of this chapter help you become a better leader?

What steps do you need to take next?

Honey or Vinegar?

A cheerful disposition is good for your health;
gloom and doom leave you bone-tired.
—Proverbs 17:22

Have you heard the story about a mother and daughter who went shopping together near Christmas? The mother really had a lot to do but the shopping had to be finished, so she reluctantly went anyway. It was one of those days when there was too much to do and not enough hours to do it all. Everyone else in the town seemed to be doing last-minute buying too, so the stores were crowded, the lines were long, and salesclerks were overwhelmed by the volume of sales. It took a particularly long time to make their purchases in one department store, but finally the shopping team found themselves out on the sidewalk dodging more hurrying people. The mother turned to her daughter in I'm-on-my-last-nerve frustration and said, "Did you see the nasty look that clerk gave me in there?" Her teenage daughter looked her right in the eyes (as only a teen daughter can do) and replied, "Mom, you had that look when you went in!"

Attitude—an eight-letter word that means "an inward feeling expressed by behavior. Synonyms for *attitude* are *outlook, stance, viewpoint,* and *way of thinking. Stance* is a posture or a pose, which in a thesaurus leads to *masquerade* then to *deception* and *cover-up.* So, then, is an attitude an attempt at deception? We think our attitudes are concealed, but our behavior reveals them as the less-than-perfect elements of our personality that they are.

When we check out at the store, we are asked, "Paper or plastic?" When we order a meal in a restaurant the waiter asks, "Rice or potato?" In the days of full-service gas stations, the attendant always asked, "Regular or unleaded?" When I make one of my trips for coffee, I'm asked, "Grande or venti?" Just as we choose whether we want paper bags or plastic ones or rice over potatoes, we can choose what attitude we will have on any particular day. Will it be honey or vinegar? It is a choice to let our words drip with sarcasm or flow sweetly from our mouths like honey. Honey has been chosen to represent the subject of this chapter, because we usually connect it with good-tasting food. Keep in mind that, as women, our attitudes cannot be phony because even if no adult spots the phoniness right away, our preschoolers or teenagers will and so will your non-Christian friend.

All too often, women's attitudes slip more to the vinegar side than to the honey! A woman decides what to wear each morning depending on what her activities will be that day. If it's a stay-at-home day to clean out the garage, she may choose her favorite ratty jeans and faded shirt. A business appointment means she chooses between her charcoal striped suit with the lavender blouse and her professional navy blue pantsuit with a cream turtleneck. Making a choice in apparel in not unlike making a decision about one's attitude. Honey or vinegar? It is a *choice*. It *is* a choice.

When women get serious about achieving balance in their lives, their attitude is all-important in working for that balance. A key word relating to attitude is *work*. We have all heard or even made the statement, "She really needs to work on her attitude." If we are honest, that same statement has probably been said in reference to us! This chapter has been written as a mini-practicum—a time of instruction with a practical application element. It's like a workshop only it isn't in a classroom and the interaction with others is limited. It might be interesting, however, if you were to do some of the exercises or activities with a good friend. Choose someone with whom you can be yourself—someone who knows you well and someone who will be honest with you about your attitudes. So, approach the information in this chapter as you would a seminar. Expect to do some thinking and formulate some responses. Skimming over the questions won't benefit you. This has been designed to help you understand what lies behind your attitudes and see what changes need to be made.

We all need to honestly assess our current attitudes since they permeate every area of our lives. Read the phrases below and choose the one that best describes your general attitude right now.

- My attitude has never been better.
- My attitude is at an all-time low.
- I'm on a downhill slope with my attitude.
- I feel as if my attitude is a constant challenge.
- My attitude is my business.
- Most of the time my attitude is pretty positive.

What Determines Attitude?

Women's attitudes are determining factors in their general approach to life. The writer of Proverbs evidently spoke from experience when he described a person sporting a bad attitude: *"a clenched jaw signals trouble ahead"* (Proverbs 16:30). Women are sometimes trapped into leading what they consider to be a miserable life when it may just be their point of view and heart condition. *"A miserable heart means a miserable life; a cheerful heart fills the day with song"* (Proverbs 15:15).

To stay in balance a woman must be realistic enough to see that much of her situation may be of her own making. Circumstances come to us, of course, over which we have absolutely no control. What we can control, however, is our response to those situations. The key to responding correctly is to make sure that our attitude is the same as Christ's attitude (Philippians 2:5).

Whether our relationships with others are healthy will depend a great deal on our attitude. The way we view others' failures and accomplishments will appear in the attitudes we display toward them. It seems that we often become more interested in assigning blame to everyone but ourselves for our circumstances. We must accept responsibility for our attitudes. Galatians 6:7 speaks to reaping what we sow. If we sow bad attitudes into our relationships, we should not be surprised when there are hurt feelings, ruined relationships, and even a ruined marriage.

Have you ever seen those wooden plaques that read, "If Mama ain't happy, ain't nobody happy?" While the grammar leaves a little to be desired, the truth of this pithy statement is obvious. When my brother and I were teenagers, we had a signal we would give each other if our mother wasn't in the best of moods. She wasn't often that way but when an "attitude" surfaced, we were prepared. You may have seen one of the earliest American flags that has a coiled snake in its center. Under the snake are the words, "Don't tread on me." When we needed to warn each other, my brother and I would whisper this saying out of the corner of our mouths! Attitudes have a tremendous affect on our relationships.

The difference between success and failure often hinges on one's attitude. *The Message*'s unique way of phrasing things indicates that our lives can become twisted into tangles when our motives are mixed (Proverbs 21:8). When bad attitudes about a boss, a pastor, or a cranky neighbor show, successful projects and witnessing opportunities are threatened.

Practicum: From Problems to Blessings

On a piece of paper, list two situations with which you are currently dealing. Don't just write one or two words but put some thought into the reality of the problem. Now spend some time reflecting on how you have reacted to these situations. Be thorough and be honest. Have your responses been negative? Has the situation become more problematic because of your response? On another section of your paper write each situation again, leaving plenty of space to make more extensive comments. For the second part of this exercise, write down three possible benefits that could come from the problem. Set aside what you think the solution should be and just focus on the benefits rather than the obstacles involved.

This activity works under the premise that some problems can be turned into blessings. Whether that happens or not may depend on your attitude.

Even though a woman is a believer, her attitudes will not necessarily be positive. Read Philippians 2:3–8 to see a list of how believers are to treat others as we look to Jesus for our example. I recently heard a sermon based on Psalm 1. Addressing believers, God sets out three things a person should not do if he or she wants to be blessed and "*prosper*" (Psalm 1:1–3 NKJV). The first requirement is that the believer does not accept the counsel of the ungodly. She gives her eyes and ears to God's way and His principles. The second requirement is that she does not stand in the way of the sinners. In other words, she is not submissive to them but to God alone.

By this time, the auditorium had become a bit warm and we were all a bit antsy. Then the preacher moved on to his third point, the last part of verse one, which says that a person should not sit in the seat of the scornful. This requirement urges us not to be complainers or gripe about everything. The attorney-preacher claimed that God killed more people in the Old Testament for complaining and griping than He did for idolatry! He even referenced that a lot of women and men have PhD degrees in how to gripe. By this time, the auditorium had grown very quiet. Could it be because our hearts had been convicted of our wrong attitudes? What part of blessing did we want to throw away to continue our complaining, griping, and negative attitudes?

What Does a Negative Attitude Do?

Negative attitudes hinder making good decisions. We are so caught up in the situation and justifying our responses that in our haste to make things better or make them go away, we rush into making decisions. Consequently, we make poor ones. When negative attitudes surface in the office or store, we are ruled by the heat of the moment and dart in the direction of every red flag. At home when Mom is "on a tear," and overly sensitive or overly critical, nerves are frayed and things are said and done that sometimes do irreparable damage.

Have you ever noticed that when your attitude is extremely negative, every situation or incident seems to be bigger than it really is? The comment a neighbor makes becomes a major confrontation. What someone says in a church business session or during a committee meeting escalates into a churchwide issue with many hurt feelings and impulsive decisions by the church members.

There is nothing as contagious as a negative attitude! Your negative attitude may prevent others from making positive responses. This is particularly true within families. When one family member is negative, pretty soon someone else is too, and it spreads until the entire family is a pot boiling over.

At one time I worked with a group of volunteers who were all very capable. I enlisted a young woman to come onto the team and began providing her with training opportunities. At a large meeting she asked if we could sit down and talk. I said, "Sure," so that's what we did. Although new to the organization, she had made a list of all the things she thought needed to be changed on our team and proceeded to give me all the details. I took her suggestions to heart, some of which were actually good ones and implemented changes. What was interesting was the fact that this woman's influence affected another volunteer and pretty soon both of them were our "official critics!" Negative thinking and behavior is contagious. *"Don't hang out with angry people; don't keep company with hotheads. Bad temper is contagious—don't get infected"* (Proverbs 22:24–25). Be careful where you sit and with whom.

When our negative attitudes control our behavior, thoughts, and words, we limit what God can do through us. Women have the potential for great influence— positive influence. Of course, the reverse of that is also true: women have the potential for negative influence. God has given each of us abilities and talents that are unique to our personalities. With His guidance, we can use our influence to change circumstances around us. All too often, however, we become part of the problem instead of being a creative, energetic component in the solution. Women can operate from the premise, "If things appear to be going well, it is clear you don't fully understand the situation!" When we do not live and move in the center of God's will for our lives and use our influence to share the gospel of Christ, we allow our negative attitude to keep us from enjoying life.

When finances are long on bills and short on income, the car is on the blink, and the house air conditioner blows only hot air, attitudes can be less than positive. It is difficult as women to keep everything in perspective and still deal with all that happens in our lives as we relate to family, friends, co-workers, and persons in ministry. God understands our frustrations as well as the desires of our hearts and wants us to come to Him and say as Isaiah did, *"O Lord, You are our Father; we are the clay, and You are our Potter, and we are all the work of Your hand"* (Isaiah 64:8 AMP). Negative attitudes are just like a bee sting, it may take time for the stinger to work its way to the surface, but it will.

Ralph Waldo Emerson said, "What lies behind us and what lies before us are tiny matters compared to what lies within us."

Practicum: Singin' the Blues

Have you ever sung the blues? If you don't listen to country-western music, turn your radio dial to a country station and listen to the large number of sad songs played over the airwaves. Look over the song titles below and decide which one describes your attitude when it's negative. Can you perhaps find a more positive song to sing?

- "Raindrops Keep Falling on My Head"
- "Make the World Go Away"
- "Rhapsody in Blue"
- "16 Tons"
- "When Sunny Gets Blue"

Your Attitude

You weren't born with it, no one gave it to you, and it doesn't have to be permanent! We adjust the thermostat on our furnaces. We make adjustments to the television and stereo volume. When we use the sewing machine, we often adjust the thread tension. We adjust our speed when we enter a school zone. We adjust the checkbook balance at the end of the month. Why are we so reluctant to adjust our attitudes? Are we forgetful or is it because of fear that we won't be successful? Or, don't we care?

Practicum: Changed from the Inside Out

Read Romans 12:1–2. I find *The Message*'s take here on our *"everyday, ordinary life"* particularly helpful. Do you see how these two verses can be matched to the following to-do list of steps you can take to change your attitude?

- Evaluate your attitudes.
- Desire to change your attitudes.
- Use your faith to defeat fear.
- Take each day as it comes.
- Choose your associates carefully.
- Change your thought patterns.
- Start developing good habits.

John C. Maxwell in *The Winning Attitude* states that we can become dismayed, distressed, defeated, and distracted if we look in the wrong direction to change our attitudes. Looking inward, back, around, or ahead is not productive and doesn't help an individual make progress if she wants to *"be changed from the inside out."* For that we need to *"fix [our] attention on God"* (Romans 12:2).

Having a negative attitude about relationships, expectations, career advancement, or personal rights is not a new subject. Paul addressed an attitude problem in his epistle to the Philippians.

━━ Biblical Snapshot ━━

Philippians 4:2–3 addresses two women whose attitudes (we assume) were not what they should have been. Paul directs his comments specifically to Euodia and her fellow church member, Syntyche. It is thought that because Paul took the time to mention them by name they had a lot of influence in the church in Philippi. Something, though, was wrong with their attitudes at the time. Scripture does not enlighten us as to what was wrong. They may have been on the "outs" with each other or with another church member. Perhaps they disagreed over an issue. The church could have decided to do something they didn't like.

When our family moved to another state, we immediately began looking for a new church, one where we could serve and minister. We made our decision after visiting three different churches. Not long after we joined a church, I was asked to coordinate a large churchwide missions event. It involved enlisting several committees and arranging for decorations, food, speakers, and musicians. We wanted it to be an exciting time for the church. People responded well to my requests for their help, and I was encouraged.

One day I stood in the church kitchen talking with another woman about the women I had asked to serve on the various committees. When I mentioned two women's names, she gasped in horror and exclaimed, "Oh! You didn't put them on the same committee, did you?" I had indeed done that and couldn't understand why she was so troubled. Then she told me the story of these two women who hadn't spoken to each other in several years. When one came into a room, the other would leave. Something had happened in the past involving both women and their husbands, and the bad attitudes toward each other were still fresh and raw. Everyone in the church (except new members!) knew about the situation and just put up with it. I refused to change my committee structure, and the two women learned to work on the same "team" from different rooms.

I imagine this situation and the effect it had on our church was similar to the one in Philippi. The unity of the church was disrupted by the two women's attitudes just as it was in ours. Philippians 4:18 makes an interesting reference to the fragrance of the offering Paul received through Epaphroditus. He describes the gifts as a fragrant odor of the sacrifice that God welcomes. Euodia's name sounds just like the Greek word that means "pleasant fragrance" or "sweet scent." In this passage, Paul creates a connection between Euodia and the Greek word that sounds like her name, indicating that he wants her to live up to her name and be a pleasant fragrance before God. Some scholars believe Paul was actually making a pun here. In any case, Paul was very concerned about how the church was being affected by a less than appropriate attitude.

Are there any lessons for us as women today in this passage? Women must recognize that their sphere of influence is much broader than they believe or even realize. We readily recognize that women have a tremendous amount of "power to sway" in family life. Children of any age watch and imitate their mother's attitudes. A woman who is thoughtful and informed influences those around her who are seeking information and answers. Her attitudes toward life in general, and her faith in particular, will be observed. Remember, the definition of the word is "an inward feeling expressed by behavior." Your attitude will show just like that run in your panty hose!

After his message to Euodia, Paul gives some advice about how the Christ followers in Philippi are to occupy their time. They are to concentrate on things that are pure, just, kind, virtuous, excellent, and lovely. This is good advice for women today seeking to have balance in their lives through positive, healthy attitudes. Attitude makes the difference between a more balanced life and one that is seriously tilting off center.

Attitude and the Woman Who Leads

I believe a leader's attitude can be more influential than her actions. While it is tempting to blame circumstances for our bad attitudes, the fact of the matter is that we need to take responsibility for them. When we come to an understanding of how important attitudes are to our success in business, within our community, and with those around us, we will begin working to change them for the better. It is true that if a leader's attitude isn't right, she won't develop new leaders. No one will want to be caught in the downdraft of negativity and all that is connected to it. W. H. Auden once wrote, "We would rather be ruined than changed." That must not be said of us as women leaders.

> The longer I live, the more I realize the impact of attitude on life . . . . I am convinced that life is 10 percent what happens to me and 90 percent how I react to it. And so it is with you—we are in charge of our attitudes.
> —Charles Swindoll, author

Which will it be—honey or vinegar? Do you prefer the sweetness that can only be derived from orange blossom, clover, or sage honey? Or would you rather skate along on the thin ice of bad attitudes with a vinegar taste in your mouth? If women really want to be the salt and light they should be in the world today, their attitudes must be positive as they use their influence to bring others closer to God and live life to its fullest.

Equipoise—*The marks in life we leave—our legacies—are most often left not in stone or steel, in history and politics, poetry or literature, but in the lives of other people.*
—Mark Sanborn, best-selling author and speaker

God's Symmetry—*Good-tempered leaders invigorate lives; they're like spring rains and sunshine.*
—Proverbs 16:15

Tipping the Scales—As a female leader, develop your social skills, learn to use words as tools, and become astute at observing others.

Notes

Prayerfully review the chapter.

What is God calling you to do?

How can the lessons of this chapter help you become a better leader?

What steps do you need to take next?

7

"Highs" Aren't Just for Balloons!

◇◇◇◇◇◇◇◇

*We laughed, we sang, we couldn't believe
our good fortune. We were the talk of the nations—
"God was wonderful to them!"*
—*Psalm 126:2*

◇◇◇◇◇◇◇◇

Awaken the Leader in You

The gymnasium was filled with balloons! They were everywhere. It was as if an explosion had taken place in a balloon factory, and as the explosion happened, all the balloons had been inflated. Table decorations featured balloons, and as team members were introduced, each was given a "bouquet" of balloons of one color to represent her position on the team. Women from all over our metropolitan area had gathered to celebrate 100 years of missions work. We had found a woman who had a marvelous collection of vintage clothing, so we had a lovely fashion show, "100 Years of Celebration." The event included special guest speakers, music, a delicious meal, and souvenirs for everyone. You see it was a special time. The occasion warranted a full-fledged gala, and we did our best to see that that was what happened that evening. It was an evening of celebration: celebration for what God had done in and through our organization and celebration of the part women had played in His work.

As women, we have many opportunities and reasons to celebrate. Celebration usually means a party of some kind, and most of us are always ready for a party. The "highs" that will be discussed in this chapter will refer to the importance of a celebratory mind-set that we desperately need as women in today's world. The words *high* and *celebration* will be used interchangeably. The symbol for this chapter is, of course, a balloon, one that is filled with helium because helium is lighter than the air around it. What eventually happens to balloons, even those filled with helium, after a brief time? They begin to leak and pretty soon, they are flat and collapsed on the table or floor. It is unfortunate but the deflated balloon can often be a visual image of what happens to us when we don't take or make opportunities to celebrate, to create the "highs" that life needs.

Women are often the "kin keepers," which means that women are the ones who plan the details and coordinate the celebrations we have in our lives. Being good "kin keepers" we make sure everyone participates, even if we have to drag them along! Life is worth celebrating, don't you agree? Birthdays, weddings, a baby's birth, that waited-for promotion, your first house, graduation from high school, university, or graduate school, your 16th birthday, getting a driver's license—you name an occasion and we can create a way to celebrate it.

But what about the smaller instances in life? Things such as a project you've completed. Do you just move on to the next project or do you stop and savor the accomplishment? The first clear day after a week of rain is cause for celebration. A new litter of kittens (wanted or unwanted) is still new life to celebrate. Watching a child read a book on her own for the first time is a good reason to celebrate. In our family, when each child turned five years old, we went to the public library where they printed their own name and received their very own library card. We took a picture of them, which went into their baby book. A time of celebration! Celebration doesn't have to be for the blockbuster moments only. As he talks to God, David in Psalm 16:11 says, *"You will show me the path of life; in Your presence is fullness of joy; at Your right hand are pleasures forevermore"* (NKJV).

A balanced life, one that has the elements that provide contentment and fulfillment, is one that will have moments and days of celebration. Life is short, but it is meant to be enjoyed. David knew that secret and was committed to celebrating the way God worked in his life. Thanksgiving must be an integral part of any celebration. If thanksgiving is missing in a woman's heart, she will be miserable, and it won't be a well-kept secret. When, as the old saying goes, life becomes a "veil of tears," it is time to step back and examine what is preventing your acknowledgement of all that God has given. True thanksgiving cannot be rendered if you secretly harbor the attitude that "nobody knows the trouble I've seen."

As Christians we can be thankful for so many things: for Christ, for deliverance, for others' faith, for God's mercy and grace, for needs provided, for the triumph of the gospel, for victory over death, for wisdom. As 1 Thessalonians 5:17 says, *"Thank God no matter what happens."* A good model for celebrating is found in Nehemiah 12. When the wall around Jerusalem was rebuilt, word was sent out about the dedication/celebration, and the Levite priests were gathered to take part in acknowledging what God had done through the people. Scripture says that they were told to use thanksgiving hymns, songs, cymbals, harps, and lutes. Quite an enthusiastic time of celebration!

There are many celebrations recorded in the Bible. Most of them are large ones celebrating national festivals or feast days. One story, however, is on a much smaller scale. It is the story of a woman who loses something very valuable to her.

━━ Biblical Snapshot ━━

The story about a lost object unfolds in Luke 15:8–10. There isn't a lot of information given in these verses. We aren't told the main character's name. We don't know where she lived. We don't know for sure if she is or was married. Perhaps she was a widow. We just don't know. The details are rather sketchy because details were not the focus of this story that Jesus tells. Rather, the account is one of Jesus' parables, a short story if you will, that He

---

used to illustrate His teaching. Jesus could probably tell when His followers' or the crowds' attention began to shift. To make His meaning clear and to recapture their attention, He told simple, easy-to-understand stories. Jesus' parables are used throughout the New Testament and have been widely studied for their meaning and application to the biblical principles He taught.

Jesus' story opens with a woman searching for a coin. To us, today, an ordinary lost coin would not be important enough to cause us to spend a great deal of time searching it. We have more important things to do than waste time trying to find a single coin that isn't terribly valuable. Such was not the case for this woman, however. She hadn't lost the only coin she had—it was one of ten she possessed. Some Bible scholars believe that very likely these coins were her dowry (an indication she was or had been married). One version states that the coins were silver *drachmas*. A *drachma* was equal to a day's wages.

A woman's dowry was extremely important in the society of Jesus's day. Many drawings depicting women of biblical times show them wearing a kind of headband, which has coins sewn on it. This was a visual sign of the extent of a woman's dowry given by her father at the time of her marriage. The dowry was critical to her financial security in case her husband were to die. Her dowry could very well be her means of staying alive if she had no children or relatives to take care of her. When Jesus mentioned that she lost one of her ten coins, His audience would have been right with Him to hear the outcome of such a disaster.

Although today we might not expend the energy to look for a single coin, when you learn it was worth a day's wages, most of us would get out our brooms too! The woman in the story searched everywhere for the missing coin. We can only imagine what took place in her house that day. She moved furniture; she swept out the dust balls; she opened chests and felt each piece of clothing to see if the coin had nestled there. She looked in her cooking area very carefully; even checking the garbage to make sure it hadn't been accidentally thrown away. She looked everywhere even the places where she would never have put the coin. It began to get dark so she lit her lamp to see better and began searching all over again. The lamp cast shadows making it even harder to see into the corners. She was beginning to lose hope, when her eyes caught a glimmer on the floor across the room. Just a spot of reflection but that was all she needed to propel her across the room to see if it was the lost coin. There it was, wedged in a crack between the wall and the floor. This was cause for celebration!

There was no way the woman was going to keep this experience a secret. What she went through was traumatic, and her frenzied searching gave the incident great drama. All this eventually made for a great celebration because that's what celebrating is all about—something happens, drama comes in, and the ending is worthy of sharing. Jesus' story moves quickly at this point. The woman called her neighbors and told them what had happened and invited them to celebrate with her. She wanted them to rejoice with her. Her "high" was punctuated by the presence of those who were happy with and for her. Her world had tilted for a while but was now back in balance. Celebrations are a legitimate and important part of maintaining balance in our lives.

We, too, like to share our times of celebrations with others. Some celebrations are private, but for the most part, we welcome others' participation. Certain celebrations are modified as time passes. Everyone is invited to a wedding to celebrate with the bride and groom. Many return to celebrate 50th anniversaries, but the anniversary dates in-between are rather private times of reflection. Baby showers are great times for celebrating a new life. Then the baby comes and Dad and grandparents tell everyone about the reason for the banner on the house or the boutonnières sent to the attending doctors. The first birthday party is a cause for a family celebration and maybe the 16th. If the baby was a girl, birthdays after 30 are usually celebrated more quietly! Celebration is a part of life.

If You Had an Entire Day...

If you had an entire day to yourself and absolutely nothing was on your calendar, how would you spend that day? Now, before you just jump ahead to making a long list and going to Hawaii, stop to think about what you would *really* like to do. You can't take anyone with you for this day. You don't have to spend time making any arrangements with sitters or call forwarding. It's your day. Write what you would do with these 24 hours in this space.

How did you decide to spend your time? Taking a day-long nap, rousing for snacks? Perhaps you chose a trip to a spa for a massage, manicure, facial, and pedicure. Taking a retreat in a quiet place for reading, Bible study, and meditation is what many women would choose. Because we are so different, it's not hard to imagine that the responses will be varied, creative, and fun. Now that you have chosen what to do with an entire day, look at your schedule for next week. Write it down if you have to, and then decide where you can interject a few moments here and there of solitude and celebration. Celebrations need not occur with a group of noisy, laughing people. It can happen just with you and God in your daily quiet time.

The above activity may have been a bit difficult for some of you, because you have become so busy with everyday life that you are not looking for moments to celebrate. Even when national or religious holidays come, women can get so caught up in the details of the special event that they lose the celebration for themselves. Even though Easter should be a meaningful time to celebrate what Jesus did for us through His death, burial, and resurrection, we lose the joy of it in distracting details. There are musicals, dramas, family reunions, new clothes to purchase, a large meal to prepare, and the celebration itself becomes lost among the lists of things that need to be done. The Fourth of July has significant meaning to Americans, yet that meaning is sometimes overshadowed by the parades, the barbecues, and fireworks. The outward elements obscure the true meaning; therefore, the celebration really isn't there.

Memorable "Highs"

My friend and I made a date to have tea in a small village-like place here in California, a place with antique stores and boutiques and restaurants. There was soft music playing, and the boards under our feet creaked as we walked to our table. It was set with delicate porcelain china. We ordered the full high tea and enjoyed sitting there looking around as we waited for our order to come. The atmosphere was hushed and everyone spoke in subdued voices. Now, I'm not a real tea aficionado, but I loved the setting and enjoyed the company savoring the classy respite. Our tea and its accompaniments arrived and the pleasantries began in earnest as we discussed how delicious the apricot and cream cheese sandwiches were.

As we sat nibbling and talking, I noticed something that at first struck me as odd. There at a table next to the wall was a youngish man, about 32 or so, and his daughter who looked to be about 6 years old. Their tea had arrived also, and they sat there eating and talking. The little girl was all dressed up in a chiffon-type pastel dress with patent leather shoes. She even had on white gloves. Tell me that little girl wasn't celebrating with her dad! Tell me she'll forget that experience. She and her father will no doubt mention that afternoon over and over again, as they reminisce in the future.

We were all celebrating that afternoon, making memories for the future like the father and daughter. Why do you think that tea shops have sprung up all across the country? Why has tea drinking become so popular again? These activities harken back to a slower, more genteel pace of life that most women seek in their lives. Oh, it may not be drinking tea that creates a "high" for a woman, but whatever the activity, she is able for a few minutes, at least, to set aside the demands on her life and indulge in memory making. For you, having afternoon tea may be the most boring thing you can think of to do! And that's quite all right because there *has* to be something that causes you to pause and think about life, the blessings God has given you, and living life to its fullest. That is no doubt one reason God established some festivals and feast days in the Bible. He not only wanted His people to acknowledge His provision for them, but He wanted them to take time to enjoy the rich things in life,

It isn't too difficult to understand why celebrations are important for keeping our lives in balance. If we recognize their value in helping us keep our perspective, why aren't we more committed to celebrating? If there really isn't a reason to celebrate, we shouldn't manufacture one or pretend there is. However, women's networks of relationships can almost always yield reasons for celebrating because of all that is going on. Leonard Sweet in his book *SoulSalsa,* asserts that we need to live "in the moment," and that means we must look for celebration opportunities. He believes that we can go through life's minutes looking at them as a rainstorm of forgettable moments or we can look at them as a tremendous supply of highs.

It follows, then, that while life at certain times is less than enjoyable because of illness, financial loss, divorce, death of a loved one, or any number of other circumstances, if we are committed to celebrating, we can eventually find our own highs. When we lived in Denver, we led very busy lives. Money was tight because of high inflation, and I was a stay-at-home mom. We were trying to juggle astronomical house payments; keep our children in clothes for year-round school; and feed a growing, hungry family. We didn't know anyone in the area, had no friends, and were new in our church (of course, this all changed with time, but for then, we were homesick for what was familiar). I didn't see much to celebrate. There was no money to go to a spa so I knew I would have to create my own ways to celebrate.

Our family has always been avid library users, but trips to the library were to get books for the kids, for homework, or some project I was researching. I decided that since (finally!) all of the kids were in school all day I would treat myself to a trip to the library one day a week. I went for no other purpose than to browse. I read magazines and looked at reference materials that I never had time to do when the children were with me. I really enjoyed those days. I didn't stay long but the moments were just for me, and I celebrated my freedom to be able to do it. I had created my own celebration.

When women feel out of balance and celebration experiences are far and few between, it's time to do something about it. Remember that it isn't necessary to spend money or take a lot of time. The secret is to look for the small things that bring pleasure. *"Now godliness with contentment is great gain"* (1 Timothy 6:6 NKJV).

Look at this list of ordinary things and choose two or three. Think how you can make them into a celebration.

- First day of spring
- A sunny day
- A garage sale
- A leaf that has turned red
- A walk along the beach
- A pinecone from last summer's vacation
- A letter from a college friend
- Fresh-fallen snow

- A book on face painting
- Scraps of fabric
- An old calendar
- Finishing a book

A celebration does not have to be a legal holiday, nor does it have to be anything like the Year of Jubilee celebrated in the Bible. We do not always know what the results will be when we begin parts of our life journey. A failed project, a lost promotion, a canceled vacation, or a child in trouble at school may cause us to set celebrations aside. However, in *SoulSalsa*, Leonard Sweet maintains that if we look for highs in everyday life and hold those memories in our hearts, "It's the pleasures of the moment that provide consolation against the drone and droop of the hours and the days."

Memory "Highs"

Scrapbooking (memory books) is a tremendously popular endeavor right now. There are paper products of all shapes and sizes to facilitate constructing a book to hold photographs, certificates, and all kinds of memorabilia. The possibilities are virtually limitless, and you are hampered only by the time you have to put the "stuff" all together! Whether you are making a scrapbook or taking a photograph, you are creating moments to remember later that will help you celebrate. I have photos from a missions trip in Hawaii that I love to look at. One of my best friends in the photos passed away not long after our trip so the memories these photos bring to my mind enable me to celebrate over and over again.

God asked His people to remember what He had done for them through the years. Their feast days were for the purpose of remembering. Many passages in the Bible tell them to recall His dealings with the people of Israel. He tells His people repeatedly to remember so that we can recall His faithfulness and the blessings we have from Him. It will be those blessings that "provide consolation against the drone and droop of the hours and days" of our everyday lives.

Celebrating and creating highs on a regular basis will help women attain balance in their lives as they face the demands that seem to intensify each passing year. As with the other topics discussed in this book, what can be found in a woman's personal life is usually found in the way she leads. Celebration as it relates to leadership can be as scarce as it is in an individual's life. The pressures of project deadlines at work, working out the details for a women's event at church, or coordinating a community fund-raiser leave leaders exhausted. Their feelings of accomplishment are often set aside with the belief that there simply isn't time to bask in the sun of achievement.

This is actually the opposite of what should take place. It has been found that creative output increases when leaders take time for celebrating. It is easy to fall into the habit of just moving forward to the next thing on the list, the next deadline, and the next project. Over time, this wears down both leaders and followers. Leaders need the time to step aside, and their followers need to understand that this is a good example for them. Richard Foster in *Celebration of Discipline* devotes an entire chapter to celebration. It is truly an important part of our emotional and spiritual lives. Corporate celebration is sadly lacking in churches today, and Foster believes that if leadership sets the example, members would understand its importance. In *SoulSalsa*, Leonard Sweet confesses that when he was in his teens he left Christianity (for a time) because of what he saw in the church: "[B]y and large, Christians were kind people in a bad mood." It is terribly sad that he saw no one celebrating.

One of the dangers that arises when there is little or no celebrating is that leaders begin to take themselves too seriously. This can cause added pressure. People respond better when encouraged, and celebrations do that. The account of Nehemiah is a perfect example of how a leader, who was delighted the project was finally done, planned a celebration to dedicate the rebuilt Jerusalem wall. It would have been easier to just move on.

Damaged health can be a result of prolonged leadership activity with no release from the pressures of leading. When others see that happening, they are not inclined to put their physical lives on the line for the organization. Failure to celebrate and enjoy the relaxation and relief it brings can stir discontent, harm relationships, and damage the organization.

One group of support staff for an organization held an annual weekend retreat. After four years of these retreats, they approached their leader about canceling the event that year. No one wanted to assume a leadership role in coordinating all the details and planning the retreat. When questioned further, they revealed that even though the retreats were successful, the planning committee had not been able to enjoy the retreat as they were too busy being in charge of everything. Everyone had taken a turn and no one was interested in missing out on everything again. The result? An outsider was asked to meet with them to plan and coordinate the retreat! Everyone was able to relax and enjoy the retreat that year and celebrate their time together.

Balance is such a delicate thing. We as women know it doesn't take very much to throw us off balance when things are hectic. A five-minute traffic jam can destroy our day's timeline. A copier breaks down and the report for our major presentation has to be postponed. Our laptop computer crashes and our email address list is lost. When these things happen, we feel our balance sliding away.

Because women often serve as the celebration coordinators for their families, it is necessary that they realize celebrations come in different forms. A walk along the beach, picking flowers, reading poetry, or lighting candles for bathtime can all be worthy celebrations. Women in leadership roles must be alert to opportunities to encourage their groups, followers, and others to celebrate.

Equipoise—Take time to read the Gospel of Mark. Pay close attention to the instances where Jesus takes time to step aside to relax and spend time with His friends. He knew the importance of maintaining balance through celebration.

God's Symmetry—*This is the day the Lord hath made; we will rejoice and be glad in it.* —Psalm 118:24 (KJV)

Tipping the Scales—Learn to play again. Recognize there will be consequences if you don't take time out for yourself. Plan for regular leisure activities. Be thankful for opportunities to relax.

Notes

Prayerfully review the chapter.

What is God calling you to do?

How can the lessons of this chapter help you become a better leader?

What steps do you need to take next?

New
Beginnings

◇◇◇◇◇◇◇◇

Grow in grace (undeserved favor, spiritual strength) and recognition and knowledge and understanding of our Lord and Savior Jesus Christ, the Messiah.
—2 Peter 3:18 (AMP)

◇◇◇◇◇◇◇◇

Working at the front desk of the city/county library had definite advantages. When the interlibrary loan books arrived, I got to look through them before calling patrons to tell them their request was in. One day I saw a new Martha Stewart decorating book. It was filled with beautiful, glossy photographs of everything from colored eggs to French Provencal fabrics to table settings for formal dining. As I leafed through the gardening section, I turned a page and there in front of me was the most glorious bouquet of flowers I had ever seen. A huge bunch of purple-edged, white sweet peas was arranged in a clear glass vase. Intrigued by these flowers I had never seen, I read the caption, *Wiltshire Ripples*. I flipped through the book and found how to order seeds for these fabulous flowers. I found that the flowers were listed on the national sweet pea registry along with the address and contact person for the National Sweet Pea Society in Great Britain. This *was* Martha Stewart after all!

The sweet pea story doesn't end there, however. I wrote to the society, never really believing I would receive a response about where I could purchase the seeds in the United States. In no time at all, I received a reply giving me the name of a seed company in New Jersey that marketed them. I called their toll-free number, got a catalog in the mail, and the rest is history. My Wiltshire Ripples were beautiful the next summer, and my new avocation as an amateur gardener was born! That one catalog was the first of many that arrived in my mailbox on what seemed a daily basis for the next several years. This was the beginning of a new interest that brought me countless hours of pleasure as I planned, planted, weeded, and harvested beautiful flowers and herbs. My father, who has gardened as long as I've known him, couldn't understand why I didn't grow things I could eat! Maybe if I had a larger plot of ground....

New beginnings is the theme of this chapter. Appropriately, a packet of seeds will serve as a reminder that if a woman is to have balance in her life, she must not be afraid of doing something new. She must develop curiosity and a thirst for knowledge. New beginnings are like a coin that has two sides. One side represents growth in knowledge, understanding, and wisdom. This includes both human learning and the spiritual growth that comes from studying God's Word and seeking His guidance for life. The other side of the coin can symbolize new things (challenges, opportunities) that enter a woman's life at various times. Some may be of her own making while others arrive on her life's doorstep unasked for, unannounced, and often unwanted.

Both sides of this coin will be discussed in this chapter and applied not only to a woman's personal life but also to the life she has as a leader. *"Collect my counsels and guard them with your life. Tune your ears to the world of Wisdom, set your heart on a life of Understanding"* (Proverbs 2:1–3).

═══ Biblical Snapshot ═══

Not only does the account of Lydia in Acts 16 tell us her salvation story, it also shows the new twists and turns a life can take when someone is interested and faithful in learning about God and wanting to grow spiritually. Lydia immediately went home and shared her newfound faith in Jesus with her family and household. Verse 15 gives their response to her witness: all of them, including Lydia, were baptized to show their commitment to Christ. Dr. Luke, the author of Acts, continues the story by telling about Lydia's hospitality to the evangelism team, offering

---

her home as a place for them to stay while they were in Philippi. Her invitation was an indication of her financial status. Most households would not have had room to house several persons nor the means to provide food for them.

Lydia's offer of hospitality came with a stipulation attached. She asked Paul and the team to accept the invitation only if they judged her to be *"faithful to the Lord"* (Acts 16:15 KJV). She wanted them to know she was committed and that she would remain faithful. *The Message* phrases it, *"she wouldn't take no for an answer."* There is no indication that Paul or the others had any reservations about Lydia's faithfulness, but rather their reservation may have been about imposing on her open hospitality. The verses following this early part of Paul's stay in Philippi record the experiences he and Silas had when they were put in jail for preaching about Jesus. The Philippian jailer's salvation while they were behind bars illustrates their commitment to Christ in the face of persecution.

The team's time in Philippi, "the city of fountains," was coming to an end. When the city officials discovered that they had beaten and imprisoned a Roman citizen without a trial, things began to happen quickly. The magistrates themselves visited Paul and Silas in the jail and tried to smooth things over, asking *"wouldn't they please leave the city"* (Acts 16:39). Luke records that as soon as Paul and Silas were released, they went immediately back to Lydia's house.

We might wonder what Lydia was doing while the men were in jail. No doubt the rest of the team, including Luke, was still staying with her. There were probably many thoughts racing through her mind. It hadn't been long ago that she was sitting quietly down by the river praying. And now, her life had been turned upside down. She had begun a new life in Christ, and nothing had been the same since. I think it was impossible for the residents of Philippi, especially Lydia's circle of friends and business acquaintances, not to know that the people staying with her were in trouble with government officials. That news probably went through the town like a house afire! She may have been wondering if her business would survive the scandal. We are given no indication that Lydia's faith faltered. Luke ends his account of the time in Philippi by writing that Paul and his team left only after they had seen Lydia and their other friends again.

Lydia's new beginning changed many things in her life. Her focus was now on spreading the good news of Jesus. She and her family were likely part of the nucleus of the church in Philippi. (Did she know Euodia? If we could move back to that time, perhaps we could ask her what the problem was!) Lydia became a benefactor of Paul's work and ministry, which shows us she was continuing to learn and was willing to invite other new beginnings into her full life. She welcomed the road to new discoveries, new ideas, new friends, and new opportunities to serve. Lydia was a woman whose balance was restored through her newfound faith in Christ. That balance was maintained, in part, by her determination to grow spiritually and learn all she could about God and His direction for her life.

The Shape of New Beginnings

New beginnings come in all shapes and sizes. Women are experts in new beginnings. In fact, most women have an advanced degree in new beginnings. Marriage heralds the beginning of a new life with someone. However, life may continue as a single later. There is the first child—a wonderful new beginning. Years later, another new beginning comes along: the first grandchild. The first job is a special new beginning, but re-entry to the job market after 20 years is a scary experience. Starting college is another exciting chapter. At age 55 applying to graduate school—an anxiety-ridden new beginning. Your first career position is a new beginning, and the move to management is another kind of beginning altogether. A consumer first and then comes the new beginning of becoming a small business owner.

New beginnings come in all shapes and sizes. They come to women throughout their lives. Age has little bearing on their arrival. Newspaper stories tell: "The blushing bride was 68" and "She was a grandmother at 36." The knowledge/learning side of the coin isn't limited to a type, a personality, an age, or an economic status. New beginnings are actually a heart issue, a mind-set if you will.

I remember hearing (or reading) the story of a woman burdened with what she described as her dreary life. She was discontented and very unhappy, yet she exhibited no desire to seek new ideas or anything out of the ordinary. Summertime came and the family prepared for their annual camping trip. Being in the outdoors away from her daily activities did nothing to dispel the woman's sense of futility. One day while everyone in her family was pursuing their outdoor activities, she walked out of the camp. When she got to the campground gate, she just kept walking. She walked away from her husband, her children, and life as she had known it. She had made the decision to start over. She found a job and a place to live in a small community for her new adventure, her new lease on life. Not too much time lapsed before she woke up one morning to the realization that the same old feelings of discontentment had surfaced again. Nothing had changed except her location. She had really not made a new beginning at all.

The Bible is very clear that God wants us to grow spiritually in Christ. Like babies we are to yearn for spiritual milk (1 Peter 2:2). The writer of Proverbs admonishes everyone to *"Write this at the top of your list: Get Understanding!"* (Proverbs 4:7). Growing spiritually is something every woman should desire and work toward. Many women's groups focus on coping with life issues (something that is needed in our society today). Some focus groups research how they can break through the "glass ceiling" (this has its place in some arenas). Other groups endeavor to help women work on their self-esteem (which can be beneficial).

These efforts to "fix" our lives can be useless to a woman, however, if the spiritual problems in her life are not addressed. What is drastically needed is a concentrated effort to help women increase their understanding of how God wants to use them in His kingdom work. What will be the result of focusing on this side of the new beginnings coin? *"So, join the company of good men and women, keep your feet on the tried-and-true paths. It's the men* (and women) *who walk straight who will settle this land; the women with integrity who will last here"* (Proverbs 2:20, emphasis added by author).

New Beginnings in Learning:
God Wants Us to Learn

When we think about how learning can lead us to new beginnings, there are three things we should keep in mind. First, God wants us to learn. Specialized training, seminars, workshops, online courses, adult education, on-the-job training are all helpful and the list goes on and on. God is pleased when women continue to learn and satisfy their curiosity.

Paul spoke of the knowledge he had obtained in 2 Corinthians 11:6, *"[I am] not [unskilled] in knowledge"* (AMP). We can think of many examples of learners in the Bible—Jesus' disciples, Timothy, Priscilla, Phoebe, and Lydia. The psalmist asks for knowledge, and Proverbs is full of sayings about the value of learning and knowledge. *"Wise men and women are always learning, always listening for fresh insights"* (Proverbs 18:15).

Second, God wants us to use what we learn. The goals women set for their advanced training or higher education need to be connected to application. As we study and learn, we come to new understandings, which may lead to change. Change is not something we usually seek out. The challenge of learning is to do more than is required for passing a course or developing a skill. The challenge comes when we seek to understand how God wants us to use our newly acquired knowledge.

Third, God wants all learning to point to Him. Hosea 6:3 says, *"Let us be zealous to know the Lord"* (AMP). Proverbs 16:9 tells us how God wants to direct our steps. When women increase their knowledge, whether it is related to their work, their church life, or personal skills, they need to realize that God wants that learning, those new skills to bring Him glory. Read Ecclesiastes 12:12–13 for God's warning about learning and God's character.

Learning is not compulsory, but neither is survival.
—W. Edwards Deming, American statistician

New Beginnings in Mentoring:
God Wants Us to Mentor

Bobb Biehl in *Mentoring* defines mentoring as "the relational glue that can hold our generation to the last and to the next." My mother-in-law was forced into the workforce when her husband died. She had few marketable skills and could find only a job as a file clerk, which did not pay enough to support her young children. A friend convinced her that she needed to learn to type. Although she could not afford it, she rented a typewriter and with her friend's mentoring, taught herself to type. Advancement came quickly, and she was able to take care of her children—all because of the encouragement of a friend. In a Christian context, mentoring is a dynamic relationship that allows one person to help another to increase in awareness and understanding of God's grace in her life.

There are multiple examples of mentoring relationships in the Bible, indicating that such relationships are desirable, beneficial, and blessed by God. Who in the Bible comes immediately to your mind when mentoring is mentioned? Paul and Timothy are probably named first. Ruth and Naomi come in second place perhaps. Elizabeth, Mary, Jesus and His disciples make it to everyone's list too. Many new beginnings in women's lives have occurred because someone mentored them. The relationships that have been formed have helped women not only grow spiritually but develop abilities that help them in other areas of their lives.

It is not always easy for women to find mentors. While mentoring used to be a natural part of our society, that is no longer true. Our mobile lifestyles hinder the mentoring that used to occur within families, and formal education has largely replaced apprenticeships. It is nothing unusual for parents, children, and grandparents to be separated by thousands of miles. Women just beginning their married lives or careers have little or no known options to acquire a mentor. Unfortunately, many mature women, even in churches, feel little or no compulsion or interest in becoming a mentor. There is a hesitancy to initiate a mentoring relationship on both sides. The needy woman doesn't know how to ask, and the experienced woman isn't sure how to volunteer! When a woman needs mentoring and does not receive it, she has missed an opportunity for a new beginning.

In doing research for a graduate course, I sought information about women and mentoring. I was surprised (although I shouldn't have been) to discover that in virtually every field I investigated there was a dearth of mentors for women. Even formal mentoring programs many times left women out because there weren't enough women in upper management interested in mentoring. I found books and studies on women in library science, mathematics, nursing, and education. All the studies revealed that women wanted to be mentored, but that mentors were difficult to enlist.

I am familiar with one nationwide ministry designed to help women break the cycle of poverty that has at its base a very strong emphasis on Christian mentoring. The ministry coordinators enlist mentors who agree to work with the clients for one or two years. Since the mentoring component is foundational to the ministry, some ministry sites have had to close because mentors could not be found. What a sad commentary on the Christian community! Women who are interested in making new beginnings are being hampered by the unwillingness of sisters in Christ to mentor them. Hmmm, what's wrong with this picture?

True mentoring, mentoring that is committed to helping a woman initiate new beginnings in her life, will consist of several things. Encouragement will be a dynamic element as the mentor verbally affirms the mentee (the one being mentored). Though some mentoring relationships may focus only on spiritual growth, there are other areas for mentoring as well. Women are not one dimensional, therefore, neither are their needs. Some may be young and need encouragement in their marriage relationship. A woman with a newborn may need practical advice on child rearing. Emilie Barnes, a California author who has an influential ministry, writes that many women desperately need help with the everyday issues of keeping house, cooking, and parenting. This, too, can be a mentoring issue.

A mentor also teaches. Teaching by example and verbal instruction are valuable for a woman who believes God is asking her to learn a new skill or fine-tune her abilities in some area. We know God uses the skills we develop for His glory wherever we are. That newly acquired computer knowledge or the course you take in Spanish may be the next step in the new beginning He has planned for you. Virtually every woman has a built-in opportunity to mentor a young member of her family. It may be as an older sister, an aunt, a grandmother, or as a mom. No woman has to go very far to find an opportunity to teach another woman.

A mentor often serves as an advisor in the mentoring relationship. The advice may be personal, correcting an attitude, or helping to refine an interpersonal relationship. The mentor may show by her example the very thing that the mentee may need to overcome a major hurdle in her life. Lois Flowers in her book, *Women, Faith, and Work*, says that women should have a group of friends (mentors) who can offer personal and professional advice and prayer support.

Last, a mentor serves. She serves with her attitude, her expertise, and most important, by her example. A servant mind-set is critical for the mentee to understand, but a successful mentor will also exhibit actual service. Service can relate to spiritual matters such as loyalty to Christ's church, Bible study, and faithfulness to God, as well as reaching out to others in love.

I doubt there would be a heated debate about the need for and the benefits of mentoring. There is a lot of discussion in many circles, however, about the scarcity of mentors for women. *"As iron sharpens iron, so one person sharpens another"* (Proverbs 27:17 TNIV). No woman can grow alone. It certainly is an indictment that even Christian women seem reluctant to step forward and help other women achieve balance in their lives and be ready for the new beginnings God has planned for them.

New Beginnings in Life:
God Wants to Use the Seasons of a Woman's Life

Turn that coin over now and look at this side with fresh eyes. If the coin seems heavier, it could be that even though a woman needs to learn, grow spiritually, and be mentored, life intervenes. Her world is constantly changing, shifting over and over with each stage of life, and she sees no possibility of new beginnings. Could it be that she just needs to be taught to recognize the possibilities as they come?

Much has been said about the seasons of a woman's life. We are all familiar with the chronological assignments to spring, summer, fall, and winter. New beginnings need not come only when a woman is young and energetic. The spring of a woman's life can come to her at any age. Spring may come later in life with a second marriage after years of being a widow or after being a woman who has always been single. Spring can arrive with new responsibilities in the workplace. Spring may burst upon the scene as an educational opportunity to finish college or start work on a graduate degree.

On more than one occasion, my eclectic reading habits have gotten me into trouble. I have embarked on more than one new beginning thanks to ideas I've found in a how-to article, a biography, or a research paper about a new approach to training leaders. Several years ago, during my "new beginning" gardening stage, I was looking through a women's magazine that had a feature article on women entrepreneurs. The more I read, the more excited I became. I took the magazine to a friend of mine, and with no comment other than, "Read this and tell me what you see," I gave it to her. After several days, I could wait no longer. I called her. "Well, what did you see?" Somewhat used to my flights of fancy, she kept quiet because she knew her silence would "egg" me on. "Didn't you see you and me?" A weaker reply came this time, "What?" I went on to summarize the article focusing on women who had started small businesses. I could just see us doing something similar in our town.

The result of that article was The Changing Vine, a home decor shop. We poured our creative juices into our small storefront and loved every facet of purchasing merchandise and displaying it. Our landlord raised the rent on our space, which forced us out of business several months later, but I never regretted the energy and time we put into our mid-life new beginning. We learned a lot about business, about ourselves, and each other. We were businesswomen who had an idea and were willing to take advantage of an opportunity to expand our horizons.

Not all new beginnings are the result of pleasant circumstances. Every year women are forced to return to work because of family financial reversals, divorce, or the death of a spouse. When this happens, it is difficult to view these forced transitions as new beginnings. With time, however, God can give us a different perspective and allow us to understand how His hand is leading at every turn. *"Grow a wise heart—you'll do yourself a favor; keep a clear head—you'll find a good life"* (Proverbs 19:8). Adversity impacts our life, throwing us off balance, but beyond the adversity lies opportunity.

Every woman has springs of new beginnings that move her either away from winter or toward summer. These new beginnings take many forms—new careers, new relationships, a move, or other kinds of life adventures. If women are to grow spiritually, emotionally, and psychologically, they must prepare for these new beginnings. If they are prepared, they will understand that there are two sides to the coin of every new beginning. Both sides must be seen. One side teaches growth in human knowledge and in the knowledge of God. The other side of the coin represents new opportunities such as mentoring and the various "springs" that occur in every individual's life.

A Reality Check for New Beginnings

Do you have any kind of plan for personal growth? (This may involve taking classes, learning a new skill, getting a mentor, etc.) Be specific.

Whose name comes to your mind in your office, your neighborhood, your church, or your volunteer service organization when you think of someone you admire and could ask to be your mentor?

Can you think of a woman in your office, your church, your neighborhood, or your service organization with whom you can share your knowledge as a mentor?

What are you willing to do to keep on growing? Be specific.

Is your life an example others will want to follow? In what ways?

What price do you think you'll have to pay to be effective as a leader? (Oh yes, there's a price!)

The best leaders are those who have an appetite for learning and are willing to work on themselves.
—Linda A. Hill, "Are We Preparing Ourselves to Lead," in *The Difference "Difference" Makes: Women and Leadership*, edited by Deborah L. Rhode

New Beginnings for a Leader

For a gardener, new beginnings come several times a year. If you are too busy to plant a garden in the spring, there's always a summer or fall garden, depending on where you live. If the weather is too rainy in early spring, you may have the chance to plant tomato seedlings later and still harvest some juicy fruit. Being a Texan, my father believes in large gardens and is not satisfied with small batches of okra or a medium "mess" of beans. Plums and peaches should be good-sized, juicy, and ready to eat on schedule. Planting a garden doesn't just happen when a gardener wakes up some morning and decides to plant the seeds he ordered or bought at the nursery.

There is a process that must happen in order for a garden to be one that will come with bragging rights. There are many steps between buying seeds and harvesting the bounty; however, only three will be highlighted here to illustrate what must also happen in a woman's life regarding new leadership beginnings. The first step is to *plan*. There is a strategy to planting a garden, and a lot of thought must go into it. When I was at the height of my country gardening days, I made detailed plans for each season's garden. Why? For instance, as the growing seasons change, the heights of various plants make a huge difference. If the seeds for tall summer plants are sown in front of the shorter spring blooming ones, those beautiful carnations will be hidden behind the Shasta daisies!

Women need to make plans for growing as leaders too. Experienced leaders can play a mentoring role in helping new ones train for their positions. Women, who want new beginnings for their leadership roles, need a plan.

Once a plan has been made, *plant*! Planting is "old hat" enough that everyone knows a gardener prepares the soil before actually planting the seeds. Having watched my father plant thousands of cantaloupe, peppers, tomatoes, string beans, and black-eyed peas, I know that planting isn't a simple matter of digging a small hole and dropping a seed in. Tilling, fertilizing, and supplementing the soil precede the actual seed planting.

Preparing the "soil" of a woman's life for leadership is just as important as the planning stage. Providing training opportunities and guiding her in developing her skills are parts of the planting stage. It becomes the responsibility of leadership teams, mentors, and others interested in her leadership capabilities to prepare her for her new role.

Every gardener's eyes sparkle when they give you a tour of their garden, regardless of its size. The planning and planting have resulted in *growth*. The gardener's interest at this point is focused on the end results. Everything prior to this time has been in anticipation of this moment. "Look at these tomatoes! Aren't they beauties? And see here, what about these green beans? We'll have enough for lunch tomorrow." The end result is worth the long hours of planning, searching for seed, tilling, fertilizing, and the backbreaking work of planting the seeds. It's time to harvest!

Growth as a leader is the ultimate goal for any woman wanting new beginnings in her leadership. Listen to a mentor describe her mentee, "Did you see how she handled that meeting? Hasn't she grown in her presentation skills? I'm so proud that she is now mentoring someone else!"

Let's apply the *plan-plant-grow* sequence to women's leadership in three areas.

Leadership Approach
To *plan* involves evaluating your behavior, attitudes, and values. It means a woman must analyze her approach to working with others and the way she maintains her relationships with them. God wants us to have teachable spirits.

Plant sound leadership techniques in a woman's leadership life. She needs to learn to be flexible, curious, and willing to change.

Grow a woman as a leader by helping her develop the ability to set priorities, articulate the purpose of the group or organization, direct planning, and focus on the strengths of her team/co-workers.

Leadership Expertise
There must be a *plan* to provide training opportunities for women wanting to engage in the new beginnings of leadership. Think about this: perhaps fewer women step up to lead because experienced leaders are not willing to invest the time or do something new.

Plant new ideas, creative solutions, and encouragement in women interested in leadership. They are the future of your ministry group, the local volunteer organization, your church's education program, and the generation coming after *them*.

Grow women as leaders by acknowledging their background and experiences. Recognize their leadership abilities will be formed to a great extent by their ability to draw from these experiences for positive results.

Leadership Roles
Plan to challenge women who have never been leaders to walk with you as you lead. Because mentors for women are sorely absent today, make the commitment to work with one woman each year. Ask her to walk alongside you and observe. If you have accepted your first leadership position and don't know where to turn for help, find someone already serving in some leadership capacity and see what advice she can give you. (She does not have to be in the same organization.)

Plant yourself in every learning opportunity that comes near you and take advantage of training events, seminars, online tutorials, and resources that will help you develop the skills you will need to lead effectively.

Grow as much as you can by having a curiosity about your new (or newly defined) leadership role. Find out the specific expectations for the role, what resources you will have, and be sure you have a clear understanding of the purpose of your group, team, organization, or project.

New beginnings, coins, and gardens. Quite a mixture! How predictable and boring life would be without seasons of new beginnings. New relationships, new directions, new responsibilities—newness is exciting but also unnerving. A woman's commitment to learning about God and His will for her life is in line with His desire that she be curious and make learning a lifetime occupation. Women who desire balance in their leadership roles will recognize the value of planning, planting, and growing in their skills, outlook, and commitment to quality leadership.

Equipoise—*Leadership is the ability to get extraordinary achievement from ordinary people.*
—Bryan Tracy, consultant, author, and speaker

God's Symmetry—*If you stop learning, you will forget what you already know.*
—Proverbs 19:27 (CEV)

Tipping the Scales—*In the end, it is important to remember that we cannot become what we need to be by remaining what we are.*
—Max De Pree, quoted in John C. Maxwell's *Developing the Leader Within You*

Notes

Prayerfully review the chapter.

What is God calling you to do?

How can the lessons of this chapter help you become a better leader?

What steps do you need to take next?

Two Pounds, Please!

◇◇◇◇◇◇◇◇

*Conduct yourselves that your manner of life
will be worthy of the good news.*
—Philippians 1:27 (AMP)

◇◇◇◇◇◇◇◇

Of chocolate, that is! No one said it better than Forrest Gump, "Life is like a box of chocolates." There are few finer things in life than an assortment of chocolates. A medium-sized box showed up on my doorstep not very long ago. I saw that it was from my oldest son, but I couldn't imagine what he'd be sending to me nor why. Then it dawned on me it was not too far from Mother's Day. Could that be it? Had he actually thought that far ahead? When I opened the box and began sorting through the packing materials, I found two ice packs. By this time, I had a glimmer of what I thought it could be. Oh, I do love that boy! A beautiful box of See's candy— a perfect choice for one of the original chocoholics. The box of candy contained a lovely assortment of nuts and chews, some of my favorites. Actually, if it has milk chocolate on it, it's one of my favorites.

The possibilities of candy assortments are endless. The *variety* is astounding. There are nuts, toffees, chews, fondant centers, nougat, special centers for spring with apricot, coconut, and raspberry centers. Then, of course, there is a *variety* of chocolate: milk, dark, white. Several years ago, I led a women's retreat and we built the entire theme around chocolate. Everyone brought her favorite kind of chocolate to eat and share. It was an enjoyable time as we sat around for two days sampling all the *varieties*.

I learned a lot about the wide variety of choices in candy making when I became friends with a woman I met after moving out of state. She and I formed a chocolate alliance: she made the candy and I ate it! She had been selling her candy at craft sales and while that was fun and somewhat profitable, she wanted a broader selling base. We went to the local mall (the only one in town), and spoke with the manager. Because there was no candy store in the mall, it would not be a violation of lease agreements if she were to sell out in the middle of the mall. So, for a year on special holiday occasions, she would make boxes and boxes of confections, and I would make marketing plans and design displays.

We enjoyed our time together, met a lot of nice people, and sold pounds and pounds of candy. Since we had formed a confectionery alliance, I refused any payment for my hours of work. I asked only that any remuneration be given to me in chocolate. Imagine that—being paid in chocolate. Talk about a dream job! My favorite payment came as my friend found a new candy mold—a box form. She used the heart-shaped box for Valentine's Day. The box and its lid were made entirely from chocolate and to top off this *pièce de résistance*, she filled the box with a variety of hand-molded chocolates with different cream centers. That paycheck stands out in my mind to this day as my most rewarding and appreciated!

Why all this talk about chocolate? Chocolate is a perfect illustration of the *variety* we have, and need, in our lives. God in His infinite wisdom created a world full of variety for our enjoyment. That variety provides countless opportunities for exciting experiences, unusual relationships, unique ministries, and extreme personal growth. What would our lives look like if they had no variety?

I looked up *variety* on my computer's thesaurus and searched for antonyms instead of synonyms. My search led me from *variety* to *likeness*, *similarity*, *resemblance*. Then the lines became more blurred and I saw words like *sameness*, *flatness*, *dullness*, and *tedium*. *Languor* and *torpor* and *slowness* appeared on the screen. Finally, I arrived at *inertia*. By that time, my world had gone from bright and sunny to a dull, lifeless grey. Even words can affect our point of view!

The problem: getting a box of chocolates home from the store on a hot day.
The solution: eat it all in the parking lot!

Women know all about variety. If you are married and have more than one child, you have variety in your life. And those grandchildren—do they really all belong in your family? In a woman's life, no two days are alike. Young children at home prevent any staleness of routine, because they move in and out of phases and moods. Have you ever been a member of a small group that was exactly like another? Group members each bring with them their personalities and values. The combinations are endless. When women are searching for balance in their lives, they sometimes think they would prefer one with less variety, but that would be a further imbalance. God designed us to have variety in our lives. Find a mirror (a large one!) and gather ten of your friends. Stand before the mirror and see how many of you look alike. Even identical twins have some noticeable differences upon closer observation. Not only is our physical appearance unique but our personalities, abilities, and approaches to everyday situations are different from those of others.

In order for women to deal with all that comes their way, they must be anchored in God's Word and in the surety of His plan for them. If you are in doubt that God is interested in variety, a short glance through a Bible commentary or concordance will reveal how through His creation alone He was attentive to details and committed to filling our world with variety.

The Bible speaks of dappled horses (Zechariah 6:3,6) and eagles with colored plumage (Ezekiel 17:3). Colors mentioned in descriptive passages or used as symbols include: orange, yellow, green, blue, purple, red, brown, grey, black, and white. Oaks, cedars, fig, olive, pomegranate, and sycamores are just some of the trees mentioned in Scripture. A variety of grains are listed: wheat, flax, barley, lentils. Roses, lilies, and wildflowers are examples of the flora listed in the Bible. The many references to food include: honey, milk, oil, corn, cheese, dried fruit, bread, butter, and fish to mention a few.

A wide variety of animals are listed throughout the Bible: lions, cattle, sheep, leopards, bears, deer, foxes, snakes, pigs, dogs, goats, apes, horses, donkeys, camels, oxen, crocodiles, and hippopotami. Birds, whether in a parable Jesus told or an Old Testament reference or elsewhere, are often an integral part of the story: eagle, dove, raven, hawk, quail, peacock, ostrich, and pigeon. What would the description of heaven's streets, walls, and gates be without the variety of the precious stones? Agate, alabaster, amethyst, beryl, carnelian, coral, crystal, diamond, emerald, jasper, lapis, sapphire, onyx, pearl, ruby, topaz—what a sparkling image they create in our minds!

God leaves nothing to chance. We may feel that the variety in our lives serves only to complicate things. (why can't *all* the children be neat?) Instead, it offers us opportunities to expand our horizons and challenges us to depend on God for understanding.

Life—An Adventure!
Paul cautions us to conduct ourselves in such a way *"live in such a way that you are a credit to the Message of Christ"* (Philippians 1:27).

The world has a lot to say about life. English actor and writer, Alan Bennett, said, "Life is rather like a tin of sardines, we're all looking for the key." Another quotation that has made its way into several scripts is: "Don't take life too seriously, you'll never get out alive." Rock star singer John Lennon said, "Life is what happens to you while you're busy making other plans." The world teaches us that we deserve everything we want in life. Media slogans like, "You're worth it!" and "You only come around once" echo in our ears as we seek meaning in life. Abundance is the key, the world tells us. Whether it's more ice cream, more pie, more money, or more stuff—more is better.

At odds with the world, the Bible addresses the subject of life in general from many different angles. It speaks about the length of life, giving words of instruction for a long life (Exodus 20:12; Proverbs 3:2) while also emphasizing how short our lives are. Job refers to life as a *"flower"* (Job 14:2 AMP), and Peter compares it to *"grass that withers"* (1 Peter 1:24 AMP). Others call life a *"sleep"* (Psalm 90:5 AMP), *"a swift ship"* (Job 9:26), *"smoke and shadow"* (Ecclesiastes 6:12), and *"water spilled on the ground"* (2 Samuel 14:14 AMP). Psalm 39:5 says, *"we're all shadows in a campfire."* Life is short!

Life's design is to stem from the proper foundation. Our family suffered great financial reversals when we purchased a house that, unknown to us, had foundation damage. A nightmare ensued as we discovered that the house was in danger when heavy rains came. If life's foundations are unsound, we will be uncertain about the future. The world tells women to build their lives on what works, whether that is pleasure or material possessions. We are told we can build based on what everyone else is doing. We seem to pay more attention to current research than we do to God's Word! Outwardly, women's lives may appear to be strong and sound, but on the inside things are close to collapse.

We are to live not for ourselves but for the Lord (Romans 14:7–8). Clear directions are given for doing good, fearing God, living for Him, and being of service to Him. An avid garage sale bargain hunter, I love the summer months when garage sales are everywhere. My mother and I were out one Saturday morning looking for that "bargain of the century" when we found a patchwork quilt over in the corner of one garage. Convinced this was that special bargain, I casually looked at the price. Hmmm, not bad! We spread out the quilt to see if there was any damage. Here and there all over the quilt there was indeed damage, quite extensive in places. There weren't large holes but several smaller ones that would require patching to make it presentable. We began discussing the merits of finding material (it would have to be old fabric) and then piecing it in to match. The price was right, but the work was just too extensive. We passed it up.

Later I began thinking about that quilt and comparing it to my life. I'm afraid what I do a great deal of the time is try to patch my life to make it acceptable to God. We patch other things, don't we? Why not our lives too? I've patched wallboard, carpet, wallpaper, and holes in walls. God isn't interested in a patched-up life—He wants a transformed one. Part of our direction in life is to pay attention to what He tells us in His Word and in our daily walk with Him.

Women have variety in their lives whether they like it or not, but we can choose how to deal with it. We can choose to live only for ourselves and try to take in all the luxuries and pleasures of life, which ultimately will be empty. Or we can choose to be stressed by all the various troubles and trials and options and decisions that come our way. Or we can obey God's commands and live our lives for Him, which means the variety in our lives will have more meaning and become something that delights rather than frustrates.

═ Biblical Snapshot ═

There is probably no account in the Bible that speaks to the topic of variety in a woman's life better than the passage in Proverbs 31:10–31. Dubbed the "Proverbs 31 Woman," this unnamed woman may not even have been a real person! She is thought by some Bible scholars to be an ideal rather than a flesh-and-blood individual. In *Becoming a Woman of Joy: A Scrapbooker Looks at Proverbs 31*, Sue Ferguson has written an enlightening and activity-filled volume about this woman, whom she has imaginatively named Val. It is a scrapbooker's delight as Sue writes about a joyful woman who lives life to its fullest and is the one whose husband and children rise up to call her blessed.

What would Val's to-do list look like? Perhaps something like this:

- Check on sewing supplies—enough thread?
- Shop for more wool for weaving
- Go grocery shopping
- Plan menus for the week
- Measure children for new clothes
- Talk to staff about what cleaning to do this week
- Exercise *every* day!

- Make plans for next Festival day and company coming
- Catch up on my weaving—finish cloth for John's new robe
- Make new pattern for belts and garments for spring
- Take finished items to Mr. Moshi and find out how much has sold
- Gather food for needy family across town
- Go through clothing children have outgrown for family whose house burned
- Make sure boys know their lessons for synagogue school
- Talk to John about new city project
- Go over my questions about the new field
- Work up budget for buying the field
- Get garden ready for planting
- Meet John and the children at the city gate

The variety of verbs used to describe the activity of this noble woman indicate a lot is happening in her life. Read the passage and look for the action words—she shops, looks, plants, makes, buys, reaches out, rolls up her sleeves. Re-read the verses again and note all the references to her hands. Her hands fly from one activity to another as she seeks out wool and flax, plants fruitful vines, girds herself with strength, lays her hands to the spinning wheel, reaches out to the unfortunate, opens her hands to the poor, and makes clothing for her household and to sell. Talk about variety in your life! Add to that the teaching Scripture says she did and the way she had built trust in her marriage relationship. With all of this to her "credit," it is no wonder that her family honors and respects her.

Among the list of this woman's abilities and accomplishments, I find most interesting verse 30: *"but a woman who reverently and worshipfully fears the Lord, she shall be praised!"* (AMP). While her worthy activities and her commitment to her family are to be commended (and are), it is this verse that gives us the clue why her price is *"far above rubies or pearls"* (Proverbs 31:10 AMP). Her spiritual life has not been neglected because of her to-do list. A woman must strive for vitality in her spiritual life if her other activities are to have any meaning. The frantic search for variety we see around us today will be of little value when put next to the principles of God and His standards. Variety for its own sake is small consolation for the hurried, frenetic lives so many women lead.

> *For no other foundation can any one lay than that which is laid, which is Jesus Christ, the Messiah, the Anointed One.*
> —1 Corinthians 3:11 (AMP)

As women reflect on their lives, very few will say there is no variety. On the contrary, they may feel they would prefer to see more uniformity so they can get used to things and establish some set schedules. A few times I have had a woman tell me that her life is boring. That statement concerns me because I wonder if she has blinders on! Variety is all around us. We see it in family photographs. It's evident in food preferences. We can celebrate it in cultural diversity. Our cities and towns display it in architecture and natural beauty. Women with balance in their lives will recognize that variety is a blessing from God (not an end in itself) and something that enriches their lives.

Leadership—An Adventure!

When you accept a new assignment within your company, you know it may involve some training and perhaps quite an adjustment in your schedule. It could be an adventure for you. If you are asked to make a report for your community service group, you think, *This might be fun—it's something different.* A conference with church staff may open the door for you to serve as the preschool director for the next year. *That* could be interesting! Because we are all so different and approach life and leadership differently, it might be helpful to look at three words and see how they relate to variety and the leadership process.

Choices, creativity, and *change* are three loaded words that probably have your mind going six different directions now that you've read them. Why would there even need to be a discussion of these words? How in the world do they relate to variety? Especially in the leadership realm?

Choices are what lead to variety! Years ago our family got into the habit of going to a taco shop for our Sunday night snack after church. As soon as church was over, we headed for the car and made our way over to the Mexican fast-food place. One reason we went so often is that the tacos were super cheap—five for a dollar! I always ordered two "loaded." Our daughter was small then so her order was "one taco with no lettuce or tomatoes." Our oldest son ordered three tacos with everything but tomatoes. Our second son would not eat anything with cheese on it, so his order was for two tacos, no cheese, no lettuce, no tomatoes, just meat. If my husband survived the ordering process, he asked for four tacos with everything. Sometimes if we had the money, we'd order 15 and use them for lunches the next day or for a really late snack. Our choices resulted in variety!

Because our society is geared to provide us with as many choices as possible, we have become accustomed to expecting them. Think of all the ways you can "build your own hamburger" or all the options you have when you buy a new car. How many kinds of tennis shoes do we really need? Nevertheless, everyone wants choices. When choices are made, a wide variety of women's groups are established, technological advances bring more options, and businesses create services customers never dreamed of (but love!).

By the same token, creativity facilitates variety also. When a committee or team is led by a woman who is not afraid of new ideas, their creativity surfaces and the result is a fresh approach to doing missions or ministry. A woman in her first leadership role can approach her assignment with a different mind-set, and creative strategies are developed. A wife and mother who is creative in solving family problems and keeping her home a safe haven will foster creativity in those she loves, because they see creativity in action.

Change is probably one of the most maligned words in the English language. Change is good if it's for someone else, right? Women's groups and organizations are notorious for fighting change. Now, change just to change is not what this is all about. Change needs to happen so that the status quo doesn't strangle a group or organization to death. In *Leadership When the Heat's On*, author Danny Cox says, "If something has been done in a certain way for two years, there's an 80 percent chance there is a better way of doing it." He also said, "The future has no healthy place for those who insist on remaining rigid and inflexible."

When change happens, and it *will* happen, we need to look upon it as something exhilarating. Being involved in leadership on some level is one of life's most exciting journeys. Leadership is an adventure. Choices, creativity, and change are all important aspects of that journey—a journey that celebrates variety.

Now let's take a second look at these three words as they relate specifically to some leadership techniques and skills women should have and practice if they are to achieve balance in leading.

Choice
- As a leader, you can choose which leadership roles you want to accept.
- Choose how to approach and solve a problem.
- Choose your team members or members of the group you are to lead (if possible).
- In many instances, the leader chooses projects for the group.
- You make the choice about your general approach to leadership.
- You choose whether your attitude will be negative or positive as a leader in your home.
- As a leader at church, you can choose whether to prepare or coast along.
- When you lead at work, you can choose your management style.

In each one of these instances, the choices you make as a leader will influence your effectiveness, the success of the project, and the willingness of your team to follow your example. The choices you make cause a variety of results and attitudes and influence future leaders and potential members for any team, group, organization, or leadership situation. Choices are critical elements in a woman's balanced leading.

Creativity

Because of the variety one finds in any setting where there are members/followers and leaders, there will be heightened need for creativity. Prominent psychologist and author Edward de Bono defines creativity as "breaking out of established patterns in order to look at things in a different way."

- It takes creativity to deal with difficult people as a leader.
- Creativity is necessary for good problem solving.
- An effective leader uses brainstorming as a means of capturing others' creativity.
- A leader can create an environment where others feel secure in voicing their creative thoughts and ideas.
- Leading creatively may mean disturbing the status quo.
- Being creative as a leader involves being willing to work outside the box in a long-established organization.
- A creative leader is more than just an idea person; she is an individual who will take a risk to try something new even if the end results are uncertain.
- A creative leader is willing to try, is flexible, and open to new approaches and ideas.

Creativity will always produce variety in how an organization is structured, how it approaches its purpose, and how attractive it is to those who are not involved but could be if they so choose.

Change

[The Lord said:] *"Do not remember the former things, nor consider the things of old. Behold, I will do a new thing, now it shall spring forth; shall you not know it? I will even make a road in the wilderness and rivers in the desert."*
—Isaiah 43:18–19 (NKJV)

- As a leader you are the primary agent of change.
- Leading requires that you are not afraid of change. It may not be the fear of failure that drives us, but the fear of success itself.
- Recognize that implementing change is usually not easy.
- If you are facilitating change in an organization (community, work world, religious), how you approach the changes will determine to a great extent whether the changes are successful.
- Your personal approach to change will influence how others respond.
- Changing things just for change's sake is an unwise leadership decision.
- Be wary of advice to change everything as soon as you become a leader.

Change brings a lot of things to the surface, things that might best be left buried! Old, hard feelings can reappear when change knocks. Change can be a leader's very best friend or lead to a dismal failure. Experienced leaders need to be alert to new ideas coming from the younger generation. A negative response can easily smother enthusiasm and harm the organization in the long run. The good that can come from change, a "fresh wind blowing," can bring variety to a stagnant situation through new techniques, renewed enthusiasm, and committed leadership.

> *Life is change. Growth is optional. Choose wisely.*
> —Karen Kaiser Clark, motivational speaker and author

Learning to balance a variety of situations, people, and tasks is one of life's most exciting journeys and challenges for women. As a woman leads in all of her roles, she will lead out of the experiences she has had. Some times, she will lead out of frustration or lack of direction. Regardless, her spiritual maturity should influence the choices she makes, her willingness to try new things, and her ability to change. An effective leader will lead in a variety of ways! This chapter resembles a large box—two pounds if you will—of chocolates. Regardless of the way you eat your way through the box, it will be an exciting adventure as you discover and accept the riches of godly variety.

Equipoise—*Inventories can be managed, but people must be led.*
—H. Ross Perot, businessman

God's Symmetry—*For none of us lives to himself, and no one dies to himself.*
—Romans 14:7 (NKJV)

Tipping the Scales—Review how Jesus solved problems in His ministry. How did He deal with difficult people? Were there any misunderstandings among His disciples? What was His approach to encouraging believers? How did He present His vision? The answers to these questions will illustrate how effective Jesus was as a leader.

Notes

Prayerfully review the chapter.

What is God calling you to do?

How can the lessons of this chapter help you become a better leader?

What steps do you need to take next?

Rice and Beans

Once the commitment is clear,
you do what you can, not what you can't.
The heart regulates the hands.
—2 Corinthians 8:10

Several years ago at a women's event, rather than having the typical luncheon, we decided to provide an on-site ministry project for the women to do. We started with an energetic morning of worship and inspirational testimonies by several missions leaders and speakers. Then, the women had the opportunity to participate in what they had just been told about—ministering to others. We concluded the meeting with a hands-on learning experience for all the women attending. Supplies had been purchased and tables set up at the back of the large meeting room to serve as workspace for the project.

Because cold weather was approaching (it was November), the people we had contacted across the border in Mexico told us that it would be great if we could put together one-pound packages of rice and pinto beans to distribute to families who would need food during the coming winter months. We purchased 300 pounds of rice and 300 pound of beans for the project. We worked out an assembly-line process and began sacking the beans and rice. I stepped away from the work for a few minutes and when I returned, there were two men standing at the table watching what was happening. We often have men attend our events so their presence was no particular surprise. They had not attended our previous session and had just come in. I knew both of the gentlemen so I went up to welcome them.

I asked, "Are you here to help us with the project?" Rather sheepishly, one of them admitted, "Well, no. Actually we heard you were having rice and beans, and we came to eat!" Since they were there, they agreed to help move the packages into boxes and the boxes to a pickup truck for the trip across the border. We were glad they came as 600 pounds of beans and rice is a lot of lifting and toting. Now, whenever I hear the word ministry, I will always think of that beans and rice project!

Rice and beans, then, will be the symbol used in this chapter to represent the ministry/service aspect of a woman's life. Using one's resources involves time, energy, and perhaps financial assets. Unfortunately, when ministry or service or volunteerism is mentioned, our thoughts go first to contributing money. While financial contributions are a vital part of any kind of service project, the ministry can never happen if there are not individuals willing to donate their time and abilities.

In recent years corporate America has recognized the value that volunteerism has for their companies. Employees are encouraged to participate in community service projects and are often given company time to do so. Public opinion has proven to be very favorable toward corporations who have a commitment to public service in their mission statements. This emphasis on personal involvement has heightened people's awareness of all there is to do for others and the wide variety of opportunities for that involvement. And it's not just big corporations getting involved. For instance, years ago, my supervisor at a small city library was an active member of an organization for business and professional women. It was my first introduction to service groups outside the church. They sponsored several major service projects every year and provided some wonderful tools for women in need. Women can derive a great sense of satisfaction from helping other women in times of adversity.

In the Christian context, a ministry lifestyle is clearly mandated in Scripture. *"Never walk away from someone who deserves help; your hand is God's hand for that person"* (Proverbs 3:27). Women, regardless of their circumstance, should be engaged in ministry to maintain balance in their lives. Because women's days are filled to the brim with responsibilities and activities, ministry can be a missing element. There simply isn't enough daylight to do all that needs to be done, much less find time to work outside the confines of family, friends, the workplace, and the church. Discretionary time (time that is not scheduled) is very limited, often squeezing out the desire for more ministry involvement. Unfortunately, apathy is also an issue that affects women.

Ministry can be planned in advance or it can be on the spur of the moment as a situation arises. Some projects can be completed either "solo" or with a group of others. All ministry projects are best done in person, but some can take place long distance with the help of someone else. All the members of a family can be involved in ministering to others. Several wonderful resources with ideas for family ministry are also available. A few of these are listed at the back of this book.

Because actions really do speak louder than words, I am including a series of ministry scenarios to illustrate the importance of ministry in any woman's life. The stories that follow are true examples of how women have made the commitment to minister in spite of their busy schedules. The vignettes demonstrate the many ways women can become involved and develop ministry lifestyles. (Names have been changed for privacy.)

Ministry Scenarios

Just Scraps
She looked around one day and discovered that she had bags, bags, and more bags of scraps. They had mounted up through the years of sewing she had done for herself, her

husband, and others. An excellent seamstress, she had produced dresses, coats, and even suits that anyone would be proud to wear. The leftover scraps were becoming a problem though. While sorting through them one day she realized there was something she could do fairly easily with all the scraps. She enlisted her husband to help, and they began cutting out squares—thousands of squares! Hence, a quilting ministry was born, and it has continued through the years.

Ashley has worn out several sewing machines in the process. She makes baby quilts for pregnancy counseling centers and for the homeless. She makes larger quilts and takes them to women's crisis shelters. Several years ago, she gave a baby quilt to a friend who was going as a volunteer on a missions trip. That was the beginning of phase two of her sewing ministry, as she now has baby quilts in more than 18 countries overseas. Women and their children have been warmed and felt loved all over the world because of one woman's desire to use her abilities in service. Her passion is to show God's love in her own way using just scraps.

Bologna Sandwiches

The young mother was on her way to work one day and drove through the inner city. She didn't see anything she hadn't seen before, but on this particular day, God opened her eyes and gave her a vision for one thing that she could do. As in any inner-city area, there were many homeless persons. While the people were obviously in need of clothing and housing, another need came to this woman's mind. That very weekend she took her Saturday morning and began making sandwiches to take downtown to give away. She didn't make fancy sandwiches, but she felt a great sense of accomplishment when about 100 were finished. As any thinking mom will do, she involved her children, and together they drove down to give away the sandwiches. She set up a table, and the people began to come. She gave them words of encouragement and told them of God's love as she gave them a sandwich. It didn't take long for word to spread through her church about what she and her children were doing. Several people said they wanted to help with the project. They offered to provide bologna and mayonnaise. So, the project grew and because of the added resources, this mom was able to increase the number of sandwiches she could make each week. The crowd downtown grew in proportion to the number of sandwiches that were being made.

After a time, the sandwich making was moved down to the church kitchen and volunteers began appearing to help. Several hundred sandwiches were made and distributed every Saturday. Then someone asked, "Why make sandwiches just for Saturdays? Why can't we come before Bible study on Sunday mornings and have a second day of giving?" That's what happened and one mom's personal ministry—something she could do alone with little resources—grew into a ministry that touches hundreds of lives with God's love.

Life in a Dump
The affluence we have in the United States does not prepare us for the sights and sounds millions of people live with everyday in slums around the world. That was true for Gena when she went to Guatemala City one December to distribute blankets to people living in the city dump. It is hard for us to imagine what life would be like in a dump. Children have been born there and lived

there all their lives. In this particular dump, some families have been there for four or five generations. When Gena and a friend agreed to participate in the Christmas ministry project, they had no idea how drastically their lives would be changed. As they distributed blankets, they told the children about God and His love for them. When it came time to leave, the children surrounded the two young women saying, "You will come back, won't you? We want to hear more of those stories from the Bible." Gena says the children's faces haunted her. She and her friend decided to return and work in the dump where more than 600 families live. "God designed a specific ministry for me in order to fulfill His perfect plan—that I become more Christ-like," she says.

A *Skein of Yarn*

What can happen with a skein of yarn is amazing. My experiences with yarn had all been related to crocheting baby blankets for myself and for friends having babies. I prided myself on never using the same pattern twice, and with a large circle of friends, that was quite a feat! I was meeting with a young woman about serving on our women's ministries advisory board one morning when a new ball of yarn began to roll through my life. It was summer, and her daughter was out of school. The daughter kept flitting in and out of our conversation, and finally with great drama, told her mom, "Class is starting in just a few minutes." When I asked about the class, her mom told me it was a special class led by an older member of their church who was teaching moms and their girls how to crochet.

Neat idea, I thought. Bridging the generation gap— good idea. A few weeks later, I heard through other women that the yarn story had grown. A volunteer group was traveling to Brazil to build churches and wanted to take some small gifts to the boys and girls they would encounter. They had decided on something for the boys, but they were stumped about what to give the girls. The crochet teacher was in one of the meetings discussing the building project and learned about the need for girls' gifts. She spoke up and volunteered her crochet class to make some curly hair ties.

At the next crochet class, she told her students about the proposed project. While they were interested, they said, "But we only know three crochet stitches!" "The pattern only takes three, and they're the ones I've taught you," came her response. So, the students and anyone else who could crochet began making hair ties. Because I travel a lot, I was able to take my skein of yarn with me and crochet in hotel rooms, in the car, and while waiting for appointments. It was easy to mail my 52 pairs of hair ties for the builders to take with them. The gifts were given as volunteers led Bible clubs with the children. There may be a Brazilian girl who came to know Jesus as her Savior that fall who will always remember the loving people that gave her colorful hair ties. Churches being constructed, Bible stories being told, and lives being transformed—all connected, in part, by a skein of yarn.

Feeding Those Who Feed Us

An effort to minister to the migrants who work throughout California resulted in the ministry Feeding Those Who Feed Us. Through this program, churches agree to sponsor one of the migrant camps for a spring and summer. Springtime is hard for migrant families because, when they move into a camp, they work for several weeks before receiving a paycheck. Food is short and the migrants don't have money to buy soap, toilet paper, or shampoo. Churches, working alone or with others, fill a laundry basket with supplies for each family, and then deliver the baskets to the camps. During the summer, when harvesting fruit and vegetables is at its peak, volunteers return to the camps to lead Bible studies for the adults and Vacation Bible Schools for the children. Feeding Those Who Feed Us takes action again in the fall, just before school begins. Churches provide a set of school clothes and a pair of shoes for each school-age child. All of the clothing is new, so this is quite an undertaking!

One fall, I drove to the project coordinator's church and toured the basement filled with clothing separated into sizes. Table after table was covered with shirts, jeans, socks, shoes, and underwear. An elderly woman sat at one of the tables, methodically opening packages of underwear and re-packaging them in smaller bags and labeling each bag carefully with the proper size. The coordinator said the woman lived in the neighborhood and donated four hours every morning to sort, label, and package the clothing. He delightfully mentioned that she was in her 80s! This clothing project developed from a small group of people committed to helping the poor who followed through with a new idea, something never tried before on such a large scale. Hundreds of people have been involved in this project. It takes strong men to load and unload the boxes of clothing and household goods. Truck drivers transport the donations to distribution sites. There is a place for everyone willing to participate. Several of the Bible studies have formed into churches. Hundreds of children have heard about Jesus for the first time. This ministry filled with love shares Christ by feeding those who feed us.

On the Road and in the City

As a leader in my church's women's ministries organization, I was asked to review a book about the ministry of an African American woman in Queens, a borough of New York City. Her story revolved around her call from God to minister to families in a former ghetto area. The Good Shepherd project involved salvaging and restoring apartment buildings that looked like a war zone. Each restored apartment building had one apartment that was dedicated to housing Bible studies and other ministries, led either by volunteers who came in or by a family who lived in the apartment complex. This woman lived in one of those apartments. Reviewing the book about her ministry touched my heart to the point that when our family planned a trip back East (from Colorado), I decided to contact her to see if she needed anything we could transport.

I called on a Saturday, and when she answered, she sounded out of breath. She seemed very surprised that I had called, and her response was a bit strange when I told her our women's group would like to collect some supplies to bring to her. Telling me she would get back to me, we agreed to talk in several days. She called me later and explained why she had seemed so distant during our previous conversation—she had been on her way to meet with her pastor to give him her resignation. She didn't feel she was making a difference and reaching the apartment dwellers for Christ. My phone call changed all of that for her, as she believed God was confirming that she was to continue to work there. She gave me a long list of supplies she needed, and our group set out to gather them. She had a ministry with preschoolers and taught young mothers to sew, so she needed supplies for both of these activities. We loaded our motor home with glue, glitter, construction paper, crayons, needles, thread, fabric, and even two sewing machines. Our family still laughs about how low to the ground our motor home was, loaded down with all the extra weight of those supplies.

When we arrived in our New Jersey campground, she and a student drove the church van to meet us, and we loaded it down with what we had brought across the United States. She worked as a volunteer with limited help from her church, so our donations meant a lot to her work. Our three children sat in awe as she told stories of how God was blessing her efforts to tell others about Jesus. She had even had a visit from social service workers wanting to know why her "program" was working and theirs wasn't! And, as you would expect, she was able to share Christ with them.

There's No Charge

In times of tragedy, people are vulnerable and usually very open to hearing about God. Women and men can give consolation and encouragement in the aftermath of earthquakes, fires, floods, tornadoes, and hurricanes.

For example: The woman approached the volunteer with papers in her hand. She began talking about all the forms she needed to complete to file a claim for her losses due to a fire that had burned down her home. The disaster relief volunteer gladly helped her finish the forms, encouraging her as best he could. She breathed a huge sigh of relief when he told her they had cleanup crews that would be able to start on her home soon. She began to make plans for signing over some of her insurance money to pay them for the cleanup. She simply couldn't believe her ears when the volunteer told her there would be no charge for the cleanup. The fire victim asked why she wouldn't have to pay anything. The response? "We are all volunteers here, and we are here because God loves you and we want you to know about that love." The volunteer then explained how she could have a personal relationship with Jesus.

It might seem an unusual place for women, but women were there. Emphasis was placed on the physical, brute strength needed to search for victims, but women were there too. Women like Melissa, trained as disaster relief volunteers. Crews of women and men served hot meals around the clock for days and days after the terrorist attack on the World Trade Center in New York City. Melissa and some of her friends volunteered to work under the tent right at Ground Zero. Her specific duties were to serve as a chaplain to the policemen and fire fighters as they came to the tent for rest breaks and meals. Knowing what to say or whether to say anything at all made her assignment all the more challenging. By her presence, she was able to share God's love to men and women who were physically and emotionally exhausted and looking for the answer to all of their questions.

The "where" is not an issue in God's call. He will send you where He wants you to go. It may be in your own homeland or thousands of miles away. The issue is not "what" because He will equip you for the job at hand. The issue is whether we will listen to His call, say yes, and reach out to others in love.

Ministry Quotables

Blessed is the influence of one true, loving human soul on another.
—George Eliot, English novelist

He who sees a need and waits to be asked for help is as unkind as if he had refused it.
—Dante, Florentine poet of the Middle Ages

Ministry is what we leave in our wake as we follow Jesus.
—Gerald Hartis, devotional writer

You must live with people to know their problems, and live with God in order to solve them.
—P. T. Forsyth, Scottish theologian

If you are a Christian, then you are a minister. A nonministering Christian is a contradiction in terms.
—Elton Trueblood, author, educator, theologian

O God, help us to be masters of ourselves that we may be servants of others.
—Sir Alec Paterson, British prison reformer

There is a broken heart in every pew.
—Joseph Parker, 19th-century British preacher

He who can no longer listen to his brother will soon no longer be listening to God either.
—Dietrich Bonhoeffer, German theologian

I have a glove here in my hand. The glove cannot do anything by itself, but when my hand is in it, it can do many things.

*True, it is not the glove, but my hand in the glove that acts.
We are gloves. It is the Holy Spirit in us who is the hand, who
does the job. We have to make room for the hand so that every
finger is filled.*
—Corrie Ten Boom, author

*If you're going to care about the fall of the sparrow, you can't
pick and choose who's going to be the sparrow.*
—Madeleine L'Engle, author

*We all have some dying to do. Jesus showed us how it should
be done.*
—Stephen Neill, bishop and missionary

Ministry Leadership

When a woman leads her group or organization into
ministry, there are several things she needs to consider.
These things will give her and her followers the
maximum chance for success. As you read, evaluate the
assets a leader has and the investments she can make for
maximum ministry returns.

Assets

1. The People—their abilities, personalities, and
   commitment.
2. The Passion—its power to motivate and inspire
   action (in this case, ministry).
3. The Purpose—to make an impact on others' lives
   and their eternal destination.
4. The Promised Results—God's blessings for being
   faithful in reaching out to others.

Investments

1. The People—A leader must listen, encourage, and be available.
2. The Passion—A leader must be passionate, informed, and knowledgeable.
3. The Purpose—A leader must demonstrate, through clear communication and a ministry lifestyle, the value and importance of ministry to her followers.
4. The Promised Results—A leader provides details, training, resources, and opportunities to engage in ministry.

═══ Biblical Snapshot ═══

Joshua 2 gives an unusual account of a woman who befriended two Israelite spies. Her story has been told many times to illustrate how an individual can be transformed by God's power. It is no secret what Rahab's occupation was. It also is no secret what she became.

Rahab lived in Jericho, which was a fortified city in Canaan. The city was in a strategic spot above the Jordan River Valley, near where the river empties into the Dead Sea. Key roads led from Jericho to the Mediterranean Sea, Lebanon, the Euphrates River, and Arabia. The city was fortified because it controlled the crossing of the Jordan River. The walls of the city were believed to have been as high as 30 feet and possibly 15 feet deep. In fact, the walls were so thick that people had houses in them. This is where Rahab's house was located. When the Israelite spies came to find out how strong the city was, they ended up at Rahab's house for some reason. Scripture tells us that Rahab had heard about how God had protected Israel. It is thought that this knowledge was a key reason for her decision to help the spies.

What had Rahab heard? She had evidently heard about God's power over the Egyptian army. She had heard about His power over nature in the plagues. She had also heard about the people of Israel crossing the Red Sea on dry ground. So, when the city soldiers conducted a house-to-house search for the spies, they knocked on Rahab's door too. She had hidden the spies under some bundles of flax, and they remained undetected until the soldiers left. In return for their safety and the information she gave them about the city, they guaranteed that her life and those of her family would be spared when the Israelite military forces attacked Jericho.

Rahab agreed with the spies that she would hang a scarlet thread/cord out the window, and when the soldiers saw it they would spare her and her family. Jericho fell to the Israelites, and Rahab and her household lived. Much has been written about the significance of the scarlet thread. It seems difficult to me not to see that it represents Rahab's sins. Not only did the scarlet cord represent her sins but the blood of Jesus to atone for those sins.

Rahab identified with God's people from that time on and converted to Judaism. She is mentioned later in Scripture as one of Jesus' ancestors (Matthew 1:5). She was ancestress to King David, all the kings of Judah and Jesus Himself. Rahab is one of two women mentioned in the hall of faith in Hebrews 11, verse 31.

Admittedly, choosing Rahab as a biblical example of leadership may seem unusual. Can she represent a woman who is committed to ministry, to service? Her occupation prior to the attack on Jericho wouldn't cause anyone to think of her in that regard. There are some facets to her personality and faith that need a closer look though. When threatened by the city soldiers, she had to decide whether to adhere to God's plan or to do what the authorities were telling her to do. She knew what God had done and what He will do in any situation if individuals trust Him. She, too, wanted to be in His hands.

Rahab had no idea when she protected the spies that her actions would make a difference through generations, indeed into eternity itself. She knew only that her faith must be evidenced by her actions. Women who lead must have clarity of purpose. They must act on faith and trust that God will bless those actions. Leaders are often pressured to make decisions or take actions that may go against what they believe God wants them to do. Decisions made under that kind of pressure are often not the best ones. Nevertheless, a leader must be prepared to initiate ministry actions even in the face of opposition.

We aren't given any information about how Rahab's family responded to her actions. Obviously, they had to have known the spies were in their house. It is possible that they may have tried to dissuade her from giving the spies information and hiding them. In leadership positions, even when a woman feels called by God to engage in ministry, family members and friends can become anxious and uncertain about its outcome and affect on their family. Ministry is not always convenient, is it? There are a multitude of excuses for putting it off, in the secret hope that someone else will do it.

Rahab gives us an example of a woman who was just beginning to see what God had in store for her. She exhibited obedience—a quality every leader must have. She demonstrated her faith in God through her actions—a requirement for a woman seeking to lead effectively. And Rahab had the courage to carry out her commitments—a commitment to help others, to reach out to those in need, a true commitment to ministry.

Which do you prefer, beans or rice? How is ministry represented in your life as a leader? In your leadership position you must be prepared not only to lead others into ministry but to be personally involved in ministry. A symbol of ministry in your life may be a quilt, a sandwich, or something else. It may be "sacramental cocoa" as described in Lynn E. Perry's book by that title. Whether it is feeding the hungry, caring for the sick, watching after orphans, visiting prisoners, or doing other good deeds, ministry is a vital part of a woman's balanced life. Paul told Timothy that women should be dressed with good deeds. (See 1 Timothy 2:9–10.)

Equipoise—Ministry and service go hand in hand as women relate to and nurture others. Ministry is a personal mandate, but it is also something women can do together as they put God's instructions into practice. Whether leading family members, neighbors, co-workers, or fellow church members, a woman's understanding of the importance of ministry and service will affect the balance in her life.

God's Symmetry—*Let no one then seek his own good and advantage and profit, but rather let him seek the welfare of his neighbor.*
—1 Corinthians 10:24 (AMP)

Tipping the Scales—Take a "windshield survey." Drive through neighborhoods in your city and make a list of needs you see from the car. Formulate some ideas for ministry to meet those needs, and present them to persons at work, next door, at church, or in your family.

Notes

Prayerfully review the chapter.

What is God calling you to do?

How can the lessons of this chapter help you become a better leader?

What steps do you need to take next?

Conclusion

Wrap It Up

The balance scales of a woman's life look like some-thing sculpted from an artist's nightmare. A pile of items and people representing her responsibilities rests on one side of the scales. If you look closely, you can see her husband, children, and maybe grandchildren. There is a vacuum cleaner, feather duster, paper towels, and dishes (dirty of course). Hanging off to the side is someone who looks like her boss. There's a chauffeur's hat, a gardening hat, and a ball cap. Buried under all of this you can see a computer sticking out, with a Bible next to it, along with some sacks full of fabric, yarn, and silk flowers.

The other side of the scale is no more organized. It is a jumble of potatoes, nails, seed packets, nuts, chocolates, balloons, rice and beans, a jar of honey, and a newspaper. Right on top is a pressurized can of air. To the uninformed observer's eye, both sides of the scale are equal messes. Someone who didn't know would think the woman's life scale is about to topple.

Such is not the case, however! The objects topped by the can of air are actually necessary in every woman's life. Every woman, and everyone else in the world, needs Jesus Christ as her Savior. He is the basis on which she is to build her life. Without Jesus, her contentment will never be complete, and the peace in her life will be temporary. He is the Way, the Truth, the Life. The potatoes' place on the scale is critical. The sack of nails must be present also. Representing her convictions, they help a woman ensure that her faith is evidenced in her actions and that her beliefs are in line with God's principles.

Because life, if nothing else, can be hilarious, nuts portray the sense of humor that must be developed in a woman's life. Even in times of difficulty, a sense of humor will keep things in perspective when life is "out of kilter." Similarly, chocolates stand for the variety that comes to every woman. Some of the variety arrives as a result of her choices, but other appears with no action on her part. Tied to the chain holding the scale are balloons that represent the "highs" of life experiences. Again, these can be of the person's own making or arrive as a demonstration of God's blessings.

The sprinkling of seed packets on this side of the scale indicates that a woman's balance in life depends to some degree upon her openness to new beginnings. New beginnings are often thrust on her and come out of tragedy or loss. The seeds for new growth should be found in every woman's life. The jar of honey is in a precarious location, right on the edge of the scale dish. Its location is perhaps appropriate since it stands for attitude. A woman's attitude, negative or positive, can go either way. It lends to the overall sculpture, however, as its weight can tip the scales toward a life lived with positive influence or one that others want to avoid.

The last two items on the scale are the newspaper and a bag of rice and beans. Good communication skills are the keys to healthy relationships within a woman's family and between co-workers, fellow church members, and others in her community. When there are breakdowns in communication, balance is destroyed. The beans and rice are the last component of a balanced woman's life. No Christian woman will be in balance if ministry is missing. While her life may be crazy busy with activities and responsibilities, if she is not personally engaged in reaching out to those in need and sharing the good news of Jesus, she will be out of balance.

When a woman makes the decision to work toward a balanced life, she is embarking on an exciting journey. Life is its own exciting journey, but to strive toward achieving a balance that is pleasing to God and living within His plans for a joyful life is truly a worthy goal. In addition to the normal, everyday activities all women have, many women also have leadership responsibilities of one kind or another. Not to be taken lightly, any leadership role requires a concentrated effort to fulfill the duties connected to that role. Balance is necessary in a leader's life in order to be effective in completing projects, reaching goals, equipping others, and enlisting future generations of leaders. A leader's impact will be diminished if there is no visible balance in her life.

Which way will the scale tip? Will we allow the pressing demands of everyday life to throw us off balance? Or will we make decisions that allow us to positively influence our families, our co-workers, our neighbors, the world. The responsibility is ours. May we as Christian women make the commitment to live our lives in balance, so that they will be a blessing to those around us, extending God's kingdom work and glorifying Him.

Group Study Guide

Women who are interested in achieving or maintaining balance in their lives may find a small group to be an excellent avenue to explore the ten areas addressed in this book. Small groups provide a nonthreatening setting for women to share their concerns about personal issues that prevent them from having balance in life. Informal sessions can help women feel comfortable about asking questions, stating their opinions, and investigating what the Bible says with others. There is something inviting about searching for answers with other women!

The purpose of this guide is to provide suggestions and ideas for expanding the topics contained in the ten chapters. Designed for small group use, this guide contains discussion questions, activities, case studies, and additional Bible study for each chapter. Other activities and ideas may be taken from the book content itself since not everyone in the group may have read the material prior to the group sessions. One woman may be enlisted to act as facilitator for each of the sessions or group members may take turns leading in the discussions and activities. Each chapter has ideas for using the object mentioned in the text as an interest display or "bring it with you" activity. The group sessions can be as involved or as simple as you choose. Enjoy!

Chapter 1
What Do Spuds Have to Do with My Life?
Briefly summarize the content of chapter 1 and then follow it with an interview time with three women you have enlisted ahead of time. Give them the following

questions to guide their preparation. Encourage them to keep their responses brief so you will have time to talk to everyone. You may choose to ask each of the women the first question before proceeding to the next second question.

Interview Questions

- How old were you when you accepted Christ? Were your family members Christians?

- How did trusting Christ change your life? Did anyone notice?

- What individuals influenced you the most in your early days as a Christian?

- What is your favorite Scripture verse relating to salvation?

- How has being a Christian made a difference in your leadership?

Enhancer Idea: Since chapter 1 uses the potato to represent salvation as the basic of Christian life, the foundation on which everything is built, it might be fun to serve baked potatoes at your first group session. The hostess can provide large baked potatoes, and several of the women can bring toppings for the potatoes—cheese, bacon bits, chopped onions, sour cream, etc. Or ask each member to bring any kind of recipe that uses potatoes as an ingredient. You might end up with scalloped, baked, or hash brown potatoes, bags of potato chips, or a potato cake!

Chapter 2
Nailing It Down

A discussion about women's convictions can be a very serious one, and there may be differences of opinion. As the study leader, decide ahead of time whether you will form smaller groups of two or three or if you will discuss the following questions all together. It would be best if each woman had a copy of the Scripture passages and the questions. The sheets can be prepared in such a way that they can be used for taking notes. If you use smaller groups or two-person teams, after a brief summary of the chapter's highlights, set aside time for the women to read the passages and formulate their answers. Call for responses to the questions.

Look up, read the following passages, and discuss how these verses help answer the questions below:

* Isaiah 26:7
* Psalm 1:1
* Proverbs 10:30
* James 1:4
* 1 Corinthians 15:3
* Matthew 7:24-27
* Deuteronomy 31:6

* How can these verses help you persevere through a difficult situation?

* How can the parable of the wise and foolish builder be applied to the building of your character as a leader?

* What kind of legacy can women leave in this area of convictions and character?

- Using the Scripture references given in chapter 2 that relate to leadership, lead your group in talking about what the Bible has to say concerning a leader's convictions.

- When have their convictions caused them difficulty in the workplace? In the community? At home? At church.

Enhancer Idea: After your first session, give each group member a small card with the date, time, and place of the next session. Attach some type of kind of nail to the card either with tape or by tying it to a piece of jute string or colored cord. Remind them to bring this invitation when studying chapter 2.

You may choose to create an interest center by purchasing nails in bulk and putting them in metal containers. You may find enough nails in your garage. As a closing activity, ask women to take the card you gave them and write down a conviction they have needed to "nail down." As women leave, have them place their cards with the display of nails to symbolize that, with God's help, they will incorporate the conviction into their lives and let it show through their character as wives, mothers, neighbors, working women, church members, and leaders.

Chapter 3
Laughter *Is* the Best Medicine

As facilitator, present the benefits of laughter you find in the chapter. There are several things you can do with the subject of humor in a balanced woman's life:

- If you prefer, enlist someone else to do the initial presentation. Leonard Sweet's book *The Jesus Prescription for a Healthy Life* can provide you with additional information.

- If there is a nurse or doctor in your group, ask her to present the medical benefits of laughter to our physical systems.

- Invite a Christian psychologist who can speak to the group about the value of laughter and developing a good sense of humor.

- Have an informal time for women to share the funniest thing that ever happened to them. In between laughter, prepare some jokes to give.

- If you have one group member who is noted for her humor, ask her to prepare a "comedy routine."

Enhancer Idea: Since nuts are the symbol for chapter 3, purchase small packets of nuts. Attach a joke to each packet. (*Reader's Digest* is an excellent source of clean jokes that are certain to get a laugh.) Have women read the jokes aloud before the session refreshments are served. Be sure to ask if anyone is allergic to nuts. (If you do have people who are allergic to nuts, you could change the symbol for this chapter to bananas.)

Chapter 4
Did You Say What I Thought You Said?

Begin the group session by eavesdropping on the following conversation between two friends. Discuss what the communication issues are. Enlist two women to play the roles ahead of time. Ask them to be natural in their conversation. Ask them to use their cell phones.

Marie (dials Janet's number): I don't understand why Janet hasn't returned my call! She knows this was important to me. *(Phone continues to ring—Janet finally answers)*

Janet: Hello, Janet speaking.

Marie: I've been waiting for you to call me back. What happened?

Janet: I didn't know you wanted me to call you back. Your message didn't say that.

Marie: I thought I made it clear that it was very important. I couldn't make my decision until I heard from you!

Janet: What are you talking about? You didn't say anything in your message about a decision.

Marie: I'm talking about the trip our women's group is taking next month. We need to make the bus reservations.

Janet: Bus trip? This is the first I've heard about a bus trip! Where have I been?

Marie: We discussed all of this at our last meeting.

Janet: Remember, I wasn't at that meeting! I had a doctor's appointment that day.

Marie: Oh, that's right. I'd forgotten that. I thought I'd told you all about the trip to the women's shelter.

Janet: Well, I'll have to....

Marie (interrupting): This changes everything. I was counting on you to make some of the arrangements.

Janet: Hmmm, I guess....

Marie (interrupting): Are you going to be able to even go with us?

Janet: You never told me *anything* about this, so how do I know if I can go?

Marie (rolling her eyes): OK, here's what's happening... the date is October 14 and we're planning to take the quilts we've made over to the women's shelter. We'll take a light lunch for everyone along with us. I was going to ask you if you'd be in charge of the food.

Janet: October 14 is right in the middle of Don's vacation. He only gets two weeks and there is no way I'm going to be able to participate in this outing. That's only a week and a half away, and I don't have time to stop everything and make a hundred calls to round up all the food and make sure everything is covered.

Marie: Well, Janet, I really didn't think you'd respond like this. When I didn't hear back, I just assumed you were moving forward with the plans, and that I could count on you.

Janet: Marie, it isn't fair of you to have this attitude! You assumed too much, and you didn't leave a complete message. I'm sorry for the misunderstanding, but I really feel it's your fault.

Marie: I guess I should have been more careful to make sure everyone knew about the plans. I suppose I need to pay more attention to the messages I leave on people's machines. Have a good vacation, and I *will* give you a full report about the project. Janet, you are going to handle the big September event, aren't you?

Janet: What are you talking about? !

After the phone conversation, lead group members to discuss the poor communication. Review the communication skills section of chapter 4. Listening is critical to effective communication in women's lives.

Ask members to read: Psalm 81:13–14; Isaiah 48:17; Proverbs 16:13; John 10:3; Psalm 34:11; Psalm 63:6. Relate them to life at home, in the workplace, at church, among friends, and discuss the importance of communication from a leader's perspective.

Chapter 5
Definition of Pressure:
"A Mummy Pressed for Time"

As women arrive for this session, give each of them a rubber band (the smaller variety rather than the wide, heavy-duty type). To introduce the discussion on the pressures and stress women face in their daily lives, ask the women to stretch their rubber bands as far as they can. Depending on the thickness of the bands, some of the bands may break. Of course, this is a perfect visual demonstration of how far most women are stretched by the responsibilities in their lives.

To add a lighter touch to a serious topic, enlist one woman to give a humorous monologue on all the uses for a can of pressurized air (this chapter's symbol). This can be similar to the things you might have read on uses for duct tape or a hot glue gun. For example, canned air can be used to dust the TV, blow cat hairs off your husband's lapel, dust the silk flower arrangement on your desk, reach the pencil that rolled under the chair, and so forth. Of course, it *could* be used to clean your computer keyboard! This litany of uses should be accompanied by demonstrations when possible.

In advance read 1 Corinthians 4:12–14 and Colossians 3:14. Lead your group in a discussion of how these passages can help us deal with the realities of the stress and pressure in our lives. Add material from chapter 5 as appropriate or ask another group member to review it ahead of time and bring a synopsis. Be sure she includes comments about how stress can undermine a leader's effectiveness. What are their suggestions (or personal experiences) about how to deal with leadership stress?

Give each woman a piece of paper with the following questions on it. Play calming instrumental music as they answer the questions.

Questions to Ask Ourselves

- Am I doing what God has called me to do?

- Is my life pleasing to God?

- How do I spend my leisure time?

- Can I keep up the pace I am living for the next ten years?

- What needs to change for the sake of endurance?

Close with a time of silent prayer.

Enhancer Idea: Intentionally choose food for your refreshments that are nutritious (no caffeine, nothing fried, etc.) to demonstrate that healthy eating can reduce stress levels. If the weather is cool, soup might be a good choice. Veggies with low-fat, low-calorie dip are always popular. Serve bottled water to remind women to drink more water each day. If your meeting place is large enough, plan to have someone lead the group in some low aerobic exercises. *Show* women how to reduce the stress of everyday life.

Chapter 6
Honey or Vinegar?

During this session, focus on how we as women respond to situations, people, and issues around us. Overview the material found in chapter 6, and use activities that you think might capture the attention of the women in your group (because of their individual circumstances).

In *The Winning Attitude*, John C. Maxwell says attitude "is the 'advance man' of our true selves. Its roots are inward but its fruit is outward." Ask women to work with a partner and take turns discussing Maxwell's quote. Ask that they specifically apply their ideas to leadership and how attitude relates to balanced leading. Allow plenty of time for each pair to share.

Choose a "medley" of Bible verses from the chapter and combine them into a reading. Close by reading your compilation.

Enhancer Idea: On the refreshment table, place a small poster that reads, "What really matters is what happens in us, not to us." Provide a variety of kinds of honey, soft butter, peanut butter, and white and whole wheat breads for the women to make honey/butter or honey and peanut butter sandwiches. Cold drinks go well with this kind of food. You may choose to serve a variety of chips as some like chips on their sandwiches too! Jars of honey and brightly colored paper goods and serving dishes will brighten the table. Work at making positive statements visually and in all that is said during this session. (Be mindful of people with food allergies and provide alternative refreshments if needed.)

Chapter 7
"Highs" Aren't Just for Balloons!

Since chapter 7 is all about celebrating reached goals, completed projects, and life in general, plan a celebration for your group session. Use the Bible passages mentioned in the chapter, and write a brief devotion to present at some point during your celebration. If a leader among you is retiring or rotating off a work group, or someone has received a promotion, use this session as an opportunity to celebrate their leadership.

Choose an occasion to celebrate. You could celebrate a whole year of birthdays and have refreshments to match each month. Decorate for the four seasons and celebrate each season with a game or activity that matches the season. Invite your pastor, boss, neighbor, or volunteer coordinator and honor them by celebrating their influence and support in your lives. Celebrations often occur around holidays so plan a Fourth of July party, a Thanksgiving party, and a Valentine's party all at the same time! Food and decorations should match each theme. If you want to do something out of the ordinary, go to the reference department of the public library and look through *Chase's Calendar of Events*. This volume contains everyday holidays, one or more for every day of the year. Celebrate National Peanut Day, or National Flower Day, or National Do Nothing Day. Use your imagination and create a festive atmosphere.

The information in chapter 7 highlights the benefits of celebrating and the joy Christian women can have because of their relationship with Christ and each other. A time of fellowship followed by a devotion and more fellowship will allow the group to set cares and concerns aside for a time and focus on all they have to celebrate.

A very large part of celebration—the "highs" of a balanced life—comes from the joy made possible through God's love and mercy. Rather than having a celebration, focus on joy. When women are invited to attend this seventh session, tell them to come prepared to relax and be pampered. Enlist several women who are willing to do manicures, pedicures, facials, perhaps even hairstyling. Make sure women know this session will last longer than normal so no one will have to leave early and miss the pampering. You might choose to create a spa atmosphere and distribute mini spa bags that you have put together ahead of time (include sea salt scrub, bath scrunchies, tiny soaps, lotions, and so forth). If this is too costly, fill a basket with enough spa items for each woman to choose one and pass that around. Prepare and present the following suggestions for keeping life joyous. Whether you focus on celebration or on keeping joy in life, the following ten ideas will help women understand that sometimes we must make our own highs.

Ten Ways to Keep Your Life Joyous
- Simplify when you can—do two things at once; plan ahead
- Pamper yourself—buy a new magazine; light candles; use bubble bath
- Exercise—you'll feel better and look better too!
- Plan ahead—cook ahead; work ahead; buy ahead
- Step aside—go to the beach; walk in the park; take a hike; go to the library; sit on the porch or patio

---

- Put romance in your life—make a date; dress up for a meal; send out the kids
- Delegate—everyone does his and her fair share
- Do something new—drive to work a new way; get a new hairstyle; re-arrange the furniture; clean the house while listening to music
- Expand your horizons—don't get stale; read your Bible through; take an adult education class; learn a new craft; take piano lessons; learn another language
- Have some fun—rent crazy movies; take the phone off the hook; play games; stay home and do nothing!

Enhancer Idea: Decorate your meeting area with balloons. Helium-filled balloons would be the best. Anchor strings tied to the balloons in baskets, buckets, sacks, or boxes. Put them on the floor, on tables, everywhere. Small portable helium tanks can be purchased at party supply stores and other places for under $25. Inflate enough balloons so that each woman can leave with at least one. Remind her to celebrate the highs as they come into her life, and that sometimes she may have to create her own highs.

Chapter 8
New Beginnings

Prior to this session about new beginnings, ask three women to be prepared to share about a time in their lives when they began something new. Ask them to focus on what was "new" and why they decided to do it. Their sharing doesn't have to be serious or very detailed. However, it should be a positive accounting how they learned something new, began a new phase of their life, or developed a new approach to a life situation. Their beginnings may not have been welcome at first (such as the death of a spouse), but they can serve as a reminder that God can work through any circumstance to bring new meanings, attitudes, and blessings to us. Give each woman a specific time limit and encourage her to limit the details of her new beginning.

Summarize some of the key points of chapter 8 between each woman's presentation to add variety to the session. Lead participants in a time of planning something new in their lives by asking them to do the activity below. Either read the sentences or type them and print them to distribute. To coordinate with the new beginnings theme, you may choose to print the activity on colored paper or on cards and attach them to empty clay pots (see Enhancer Idea below).

Fill-in-the-Blanks Activity

- Learn to _____.
- Get a degree in _____.
- Find someone to mentor me in _____.
- Ask _____ to teach me how to _____.
- Participate in _____ ministry to broaden my outlook.
- Talk to _____ about _____ in my past.
- Write to _____ to thank her for being my friend/ mentor.

Ask for volunteers to share briefly about a time when they began a new leadership role. How did they feel? Did they make mistakes? What helped them the most?

Enhancer Idea: Because we often associate new beginnings with growth, there are several things you could do to enhance this session.

If you choose to attach the activity card to a clay pot, plan to have a potting party after the more formal part of your session. This can be as complicated or as simple as you choose. Decorating the pots with tissue paper or paints might appeal to some of the women in your group. Dry brushing paint is a quick and easy way to decorate plain clay pots, too. Purchase a flat of annuals (pansies, petunias, etc.) and give each woman potting mix and one plant for her to plant.

If you don't have money to purchase plants, but can afford the pots, buy seeds and soil, and let the women plant those.

For another—even less expensive idea—many discount stores carry seed packets (several for $1), so consider giving each woman a packet. On the back of the seed packets attach a label with the words, *"The wise accumulate knowledge—a true treasure"* (Proverbs 10:14).

Challenge the women as they leave to follow through with what they put in the blanks on their cards. Remind them that new beginnings offer opportunities to grow spiritually, emotionally, and psychologically.

Take the new beginnings theme to the edge by asking everyone ahead of time to fix a recipe they have never made before (and no fair tasting the results ahead of time!). You might suggest they bake with an ingredient they've never used before. It might be a real time of new beginnings!

Chapter 9
Two Pounds, Please!

Begin the session with a creativity exercise that will demonstrate the wide variety of ideas that can come from a group of women. Divide the group into two teams and give each team a plastic foam cup. Ask each group to select a scribe. Start a timer and give them one minute to list all the uses for the cup that they can. As the groups read their lists have them mark off any duplicates. The group with the longest list wins a prize. Since the symbol for this chapter is chocolates, the prize will of course be a package of chocolate candy!

After presenting some of the information from chapter 9, lead the women in a brief study of the many parts in Christ's body, the church, found in Romans 12:6–8. A list of the spiritual gifts given to believers is given in 1 Corinthians 12:12–28. Use these two passages to illustrate the variety found in the church. Ask women to share which gift they believe they have and how they are using the gift. Be sure to emphasize that the gift one woman has is not more important or valuable than another's gift. Lead in a discussion about how women can discover their gifts.

Prior to the session, ask a woman who has held a variety of leadership roles to speak for five minutes about how that variety has helped her to develop flexibility.

Enhancer Idea: To promote this session (the week before), attach an invitation/reminder to pieces of wrapped chocolate. On the invitation, ask everyone to bring their favorite kind of chocolate candy (this will be a time to throw calorie caution to the wind!). If the women you are inviting will respond better to making chocolate desserts instead of just buying a bag of candy, ask them to do that. The more chocolate, the better. If you choose to use the store candy idea, decorate your table with a variety of candy bars. You could even make a candy bar "cake" as a centerpiece. Attach two round six-inch or eight-inch circles of plastic foam together with toothpicks. Buy enough chocolate candy bars to stand up all around the two-layer cake. Keep them in their wrappers and attach them with long pins, cool glue sticks, or a drop of white glue. Fill in the top with various wrapped chocolate candy. Tie the cake with decorative two-inch-wide ribbon. Give the cake to the woman with the birthday closest to your session date.

If you use wrapped chocolates, put them in a variety of colored plastic and glass bowls for a lively tablescape.

Cut chocolate desserts into very small pieces so there will be a lot of sampling. Use colorful paper products and plastic utensils to complete the colorful display. Variety is the topic for chapter 9, so use your imagination!

Chapter 10
Rice and Beans

It is fitting that the final session focuses on ministry. There are many opportunities for your group to engage in reaching out to others. Interest in service-oriented community projects is on the rise, so this will be an excellent way to introduce your group members to doing something that meets someone else's needs.

Make arrangements ahead of time to involve your group in a project. Choose one that can be completed during your session. Gather the supplies you will need for the activity. Involve as many of the group members as possible in the details of the project. Ideas for easy-to-do projects can be found in several of the books in the Resource Guide. Plan to enlist group members in delivering the finished project. This one project may lead to others and to your women's understanding that ministry should be a part of their Christian life.

If you think participants have not read chapter 10 prior to the session, use the ministry scenarios to illustrate the variety of ways women can respond through ministry. Ask these questions: *How does ministry fit into a leader's life? Can a woman be an effective leader and not minister to others?*

Enhancer Idea: Purchase dried pinto beans and put them in snack bags with a note inside about your final session. It would be an obvious connection to serve rice and beans, jambalaya, or chili for your break or refreshment time.

At the conclusion of your final group session...
Tie together all the areas in which a woman needs to have balance. Purchase a small cardboard box for each woman. If you do not have funds for boxes, use small gift sacks that can be purchased at discount stores.

Present an overview of all the topics that have been discussed during your sessions. Give each woman ten objects (one for each topic) to put in her "Balance Box" to remind her of the balance she needs in her life. As you comment on each area and hand out the matching object, be sure to connect the object to women as leaders. The application from daily life to one's leadership life must be made. The following items could be used to represent the ten aspects of a balanced woman's life and leadership.

Balance Box Items

- computer-generated picture of a potato (if you are brave, distribute a potato chip!)—salvation
- roofing nail, finishing nail, or another kind of nail—convictions
- walnut or some other nut in its shell—sense of humor/laughter
- square of newspaper—communication
- can of air or rubber band—stress/pressure
- computer-generated picture of a jar of honey or a fuzzy bee to represent honey—attitude
- balloon—"highs"/celebration
- packet of seeds—new beginnings/growth
- piece of chocolate—variety
- snack bag of beans and/or rice—ministry

Resource Guide

A Balanced Diet

Baker, Amy C. *Succeed at Work without Sidetracking Your Faith: 7 Lessons of Career Excellence for Women* (New Hope Publishers, 2005).

Burroughs, Esther. *A Garden Path to Mentoring: Planting Your Life in Another and Releasing the Fragrance of Christ* (New Hope Publishers, 1997).

Clark, Linda. *5 Leadership Essentials for Women: Developing Your Ability to Make Things Happen* (New Hope Publishers, 2004).

Collins, Travis. *Directionally Challenged: How to Find & Follow God's Course for Your Life* (New Hope Publishers, 2007).

_____. *Tough Calls: Game-Winning Principles for Leaders Under Pressure* (New Hope Publishers, 2008).

Ellison, Edna and Tricia Scribner. *Woman to Woman: Preparing Yourself to Mentor* (New Hope Publishers, 2005).

Farrell, Bill and Pam Farrell. *Men Are Like Waffles— Women Are Like Spaghetti: Understanding and Delighting in Your Differences* (Harvest House Publishers, 2007).

Goodman, Karon Phillips. *Stepping-Stones for Stepmoms: Everyday Strength for a Blended-Family Mom* (New Hope Publishers, 2006).

Heartsill, Tonya. *We Can Do That! 100+ Ways Families Can Be On Mission* (WMU, 2005).

Joiner, Barbara. *Yours for the Giving: Spiritual Gifts* (New Hope Publishers, 2004).

Kelley, Rhonda H. *A Woman's Guide to Servant Leadership: A Biblical Study for Becoming a Christlike Leader* (New Hope Publishers, 2002).

_____. *Raising Moms: Daughters Caring for Mothers in Their Later Years* (New Hope Publishers, 2006).

Kendall, Jackie. *The Mentoring Mom: 11 Ways to Model Christ for Your Child* (New Hope Publishers, 2006).

Lee, Wanda. *Live the Call: Embrace God's Design for Your Life* (New Hope Publishers, 2006).

Lush, Jean and Pam Vredevelt. *Women and Stress: Practical Ways to Manage Tension* (Revell, 2008).

Mitchell, Joyce. *Teams Work: A No-Nonsense Approach to Achieving More Together* (New Hope Publishers, 2008).

Perry, Lynn E. *Sacramental Cocoa and Other Stories from the Parish of the Poor* (Westminster John Knox Press, 1995).

Poinsett, Brenda. *She Walked with Jesus: Stories of Christ Followers in the Bible* (New Hope Publishers, 2004).

Rhea, Carolyn. *When Grief Is Your Constant Companion: God's Grace for a Woman's Heartache* (New Hope Publishers, 2003).

Robinson, Ella. *I Can Do That Too! More Ways to Be On Mission* (WMU, 2006).

Whitwer, Glynnis. *Work@Home: A Practical Guide for Women Who Want to Work from Home* (New Hope Publishers, 2007).

Williams, Debbie Taylor. *If God Is in Control, Why Do I Have a Headache? Bible Lessons for a Woman's Total Health* (New Hope Publishers, 2004).

Wood, Cindi. *The Frazzled Female: Finding God's Peace in Your Daily Chaos* (B&H Publishing Group, 2006).

Books in Spanish:
Lee, Wanda. *Vive el llamado: Haga suyo el plan de Dios para su vida* (New Hope Publishers, 2007).

Littauer, Florence. *Rayos de esperanza: Cómo vencer la depresión* (New Hope Publishers, 2006).

Vázquez, Mirta. *¿El amor todo lo soporta?* (WMU, 2002).

Web sites:

www.wmustore.com: Resources for women from Woman's Missionary Union

www.wmu.com/volunteerconnection: Ministry ideas and opportunities for women, including Christian Women's Job Corps®

www.newhopepublishers.com: Resources for missional living (missions, women's and family issues, Bible studies)

www.lifeway.com: Resources for women's Bible studies

www.WorldCraftsVillage.com: Handcrafted, fair-trade items from around the world for sale to assist women and men who make them

www.namb.net: Ministry opportunities within North America

www.imb.org: International missions opportunities

www.cwlc.us: Christian Women's Leadership Center, Samford University, Birmingham, Alabama

More *New Hope*
Resources for Women
in Leadership

5 Leadership Essentials for Women
Developing Your Ability to Make
Things Happen
Compiled by Linda Clark
ISBN 10: 1-56309-842-3
ISBN 13: 978-1-56309-842-0

Woman to Woman
Preparing Yourself to Mentor
Edna Ellison and Tricia Scribner
ISBN-10: 1-56309-949-7
ISBN-13: 978-1-56309-949-6

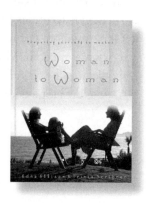

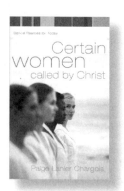

Certain Women Called by Christ
Biblical Realities for Today
Paige Lanier Chargois
ISBN-10: 1-59669-200-6
ISBN-13: 978-1-59669-200-8

Available in bookstores everywhere
For information about these books or any New Hope product,
visit www.newhopepublishers.com.